Volume 2

Mathematicians Are People, Too

Stories from the Lives of Great Mathematicians

For our parents—
Sam and Bertha Feil
Nick and Lydia Reimer
—with love and gratitude

Project Editor: Joan Gideon
Production Coordinator: Claire Flaherty
Art: Rachel Gage

ISBN 0-86651-823-1
Printed in the United States of America
16 17 18 19 20 10 09 08 07

1-800-321-3106
www.pearsonlearning.com

Contents

Introduction and Suggestions for Teachers

◆

Almost nothing captures the interest and attention of students like a good story. The teaching power of stories throughout history is well documented; current learning theory reinforces their value.

This collection of stories about great mathematicians is designed to enrich and motivate learning about mathematicians. As the book's title suggests, each story highlights the fact that mathematics was developed and shaped by real men and women. They faced the full range of challenges and obstacles, triumphs and defeats.

Although the focus of this book is on the human dimension, the subject of mathematics is treated with respect. When possible, mathematical concepts are explained in simple terms. A glossary is included to increase students' understanding of the mathematical terms and ideas. A list of supplementary sources in mathematics history points to additional biographical and mathematical information.

The stories in this book are written to be read aloud. Most are short enough to read in fifteen or twenty minutes. They are also easy enough for children to read, either in small groups or alone. Many teachers have used Volume 1 as a resource for students doing research or reports. Others have used the material in the stories as starters for student skits, video scripts, and art or social studies projects.

While one could read the entire book in a short period of time, it may be most effective to read the stories at intervals, perhaps in conjunction with a mathematician's birthday or as an introduction to a particular mathematical idea or concept.

Here is a partial listing of mathematical topics and the stories that feature them.

Problem solving: All stories. See especially Cardano, Banneker, Babbage, Einstein, Pólya

Geometry: Euclid, Fibonacci, Descartes, Fermat, Agnesi, Khayyam

Algebra: Khayyam, Fibonacci, Descartes, Agnesi, Somerville, Abel, Einstein

Number systems and number theory: Euclid, Fibonacci, Fermat, Abel

Probability: Cardano, Fermat

Calculators and computers: Babbage, Lovelace

Women in mathematics: Agnesi, Somerville, Lovelace, Kovalevsky

Calculus: Agnesi, Kovalevsky

Introduction for Students

◆

In the middle of a difficult mathematics problem it's easy to forget that every aspect of mathematics started with a person. Someone somewhere had a problem to solve or was fascinated with a discovery. Because that person spent time thinking and working on his or her ideas, we now have a beautifully arranged system of mathematics.

Descartes, who liked to stay in bed until noon, once saw a fly crawl on the ceiling above his bed. This inspired him to develop coordinate geometry. Charles Babbage observed how cards punched with little holes guided a loom to weave intricate designs in cloth. When he applied the same procedure to the machine he was building, the computer was born. Sonya Kovalevsky's parents ran out of wallpaper before her bedroom was papered. They used lithographed calculus notes instead, and she became fascinated by the formulas on her wall. Einstein's interest in science began when his father gave him an inexpensive compass for his fifth birthday.

Behind every mathematical discovery is an interesting person. The stories in this book tell about the lives and work of fifteen great mathematicians. Some of them are well-known; others you may read about for the first time. Some are men and some are women. They come from many parts of the world and represent many different cultures. But they have at least two things in common—curiosity and determination.

As you read these stories, try to imagine that you are living in the same times and places as the mathematicians you read about.

Some of the details and conversations are imaginary, but all of the stories are true. When you have finished this book, you may want to read more about these or other mathematicians in your local library or in other books. Remember to check the glossary if there are mathematical terms you are unfamiliar with.

When you understand why and how these mathematicians made their discoveries, you will come to a new appreciation of mathematics. You will also learn that curiosity and determination help everyone in making discoveries and solving problems of all kinds.

EUCLID (YOO-klid), ca. 330–275 B.C., was one of the three greatest mathematicians of antiquity. He was the first professor of mathematics at the University of Alexandria in Egypt, and shaped mathematics teaching for over 2000 years with his thirteen-volume text, *Elements.*

There's Only One Road

Alex flung his arm wildly as he erased his slate. It was the third time he had tried to draw the constellation. His last drawing of Leo looked more like a water jug than a lion.

"That's enough," he groaned aloud. "I don't see why we have to learn this anyway. When will I ever have to know what the stars look like? If I do need to know, I can just go outside at night and look up. What am I ever going to get out of this?"

This was just the signal his grandfather was waiting for. He never missed an opportunity to tell a story, especially if it contained a moral for his grandsons.

"Alex, did I ever tell you about the time I asked that question?" he began.

"Yes, Grandfather," Alex said with his teeth clenched. Under his breath he added, "about a million times."

The old man leaned forward on his bench and cupped his ear. "What's that? You've got to speak up. You know I can't hear as well as I used to. But," he added, "I can remember that day as if it were yesterday."

Without giving Alex or his brother Theon a chance to escape, Grandfather began the familiar story. "Let's see. . . . It was about fifty years ago—maybe fifty-five. Anyway, I was just a young fellow, a little older than you, Alex. My parents thought I needed to study geometry, so they hired a popular young man by the name of Euclid to be my tutor."

Grandfather glanced at the boys and chuckled. "Of course, I had other ideas. Why should I study mathematics? I wanted to work in the fields, maybe train to be a stonecutter. I figured that if I could earn some money for myself, I would be more independent. I wanted to travel and see the world!" He stopped to make sure Alex and Theon were listening. "There's nothing wrong with that, of course. I expect both of you boys to go wherever you can. After all, there's a whole world out there to explore. Egypt is a great place to live, but you need to see Italy and Greece, and. . . ."

Suddenly he stopped and scratched his head. "Now where was I? Oh yes, my story. Well, I made a bad mistake on my first day with the tutor. Euclid had just carefully explained the most important fundamentals of geometry. Then he asked me if I had any questions. Can you guess what I said?"

Alex and Theon both knew very well what their grandfather had said. They could have told the story themselves, BACKWARDS. But they knew it was best to play along. "What did you say, Grandfather?" they chorused.

"I said, 'What will I gain by learning this?' Can you believe it? That's what I said. Before I even knew what was happening, Euclid snapped his fingers and told his assistant to give me three pennies. 'Here,' he said, 'since you must make a profit from everything you learn, take these.' I was mighty embarrassed to see how

I had hurt his feelings. Believe me, I learned an important lesson that day."

Alex and Theon quietly picked up their school bags and tried to slip out of the room. "Thanks, Grandfather. See you later," they waved.

"Wait a minute, you two!" he called, stopping them in their tracks. "What's the moral of the story?"

The boys looked at each other, rolled their eyes, and recited in unison, "Never ask what you will gain from knowledge, knowledge is gain enough."

As soon as their grandfather released them, they scurried out the door and down the path to their own home. "I hope you learned *another* lesson," Theon scolded Alex. "Never let Grandfather tell you that story again!"

Alex laughed. "Yes. But at least we got away before he remembered his banquet story. We would have been there all afternoon!"

Although Euclid had been dead more than twenty-five years, Grandfather loved talking about him. He was proud to have known the famous teacher personally. He enjoyed telling how Euclid had been invited to design and direct the Department of Mathematics at the great university when it opened in Alexandria. Euclid's position had been a prestigious one, and he had influenced many outstanding students. Scholars came from all over the world to study at the university and to conduct research in its excellent library.

Grandfather had told Alex and Theon how the famous university had been founded by the Egyptian King, Ptolemy. Ptolemy wanted an impressive school with lecture rooms and laboratories. He hoped students would relax in its beautiful gardens, and he envisioned magnificent museums, which would be visited by the city's guests. At the very heart of the university would be a massive library—the largest in the world.

"Ptolemy's plans became a reality in a short time," said Grandfather. "When the university opened about the time I was studying with Euclid, its library held over 600,000 items, all on papyrus rolls. The university and the city have become the intellectual center of Greek civilization."

Such a major project could not have been accomplished without the support of the king. Ptolemy was not only a good leader, he was also an eager learner. Because he wanted to absorb as much knowledge as he could from the university faculty, he often invited professors to come to his chambers for discussions and lessons.

"Euclid was one such professor," said Grandfather. "He was a modest, gentle man, and a patient teacher who loved his work at the university. He enjoyed his students, and they responded by studying diligently. He quickly discovered, however, that it was difficult to teach mathematics with the available textbooks. Mathematical knowledge was terribly disorganized in those days. Students often became confused as they tried to sort through the muddled texts. They had a hard time seeing how one concept related to another."

Euclid set about to organize the existing mathematical knowledge. He began to work on *Elements*, a thirteen-volume set that was destined to be the most famous mathematical textbook in the history of the world. Very little of the book is Euclid's original mathematical work. Instead, he carefully and systematically arranged everything that had been discovered and accomplished by other mathematicians.

Euclid's book amazed the world. Never had a book been so accurate and so full of logical thinking. Step by step, Euclid led his readers through the discoveries of great thinkers such as Pythagoras, Hippocrates, Plato, and Aristotle. The book was popular immediately, and its popularity lasted. In fact, Euclid's *Elements* was the standard textbook of mathematics around the world for over 2000 years. No other book—except the Bible—has been translated into so many languages, printed in so many editions, or discussed in so many commentaries.

When Alex and Theon got home, their mother had an errand for them to run. "Go and tell your grandfather to come eat with us this evening. He doesn't eat well since he quit working in the king's household, and at his age he should."

"We were just there," Theon explained. "We thought maybe he would help us with our astronomy lesson, but he got going on his Euclid stories again. If he comes to dinner tonight," he warned, "we'll have to keep him off the subject."

That evening the boys ate quickly, hoping to be excused before their grandfather got started on Euclid. Suddenly he cleared his throat and turned to their mother. "You know, I was talking to the boys today about geometry, and . . ."

"Grandfather," Alex interrupted. "We were studying astronomy, not geometry."

"Oh yes, that's right," he agreed, looking a little embarrassed.

"Won't you have some more rice, Grandfather?" Theon suggested, hoping to fill the old man's mouth with more than stories.

"Thank you, son," he replied. "You know, I believe they had rice at the banquet that night when Euclid . . ."

Alex knew he had to do something fast. "Rice. Rice is a great staple. Did you know, Grandfather, that more rice is grown in China than in all other countries combined?"

"Hmm. Is that so?" He scratched his chin, and suddenly his eyes lit up. "King Ptolemy used to speak of traveling around the world, perhaps even to China, if the roads could be built. Say, that reminds me. Have I ever told you about what happened at the banquet when Euclid put King Ptolemy on the spot?"

Alex and Theon admitted defeat. Nothing could stop Grandfather when he was determined to tell a story. They grinned at each other and settled back in their chairs. Might as well enjoy it, they thought.

"Well, the servants prepared a magnificent dinner that night. Hundreds of the most prominent citizens attired in their finest clothes and jewels came to celebrate the first anniversary of the university. Euclid, of course, was one of the guests of honor.

"By the way," said Grandfather, chuckling, "have I ever mentioned how short Euclid was?" Alex and Theon smiled and nodded. They knew exactly what was to come.

"When it came to stature and determination, however, Euclid was a giant!" Grandfather announced loudly.

He continued with his tale, his eyes sparkling as he seemed to watch the story unfold. "King Ptolemy stood and introduced Euclid to the other guests. Then he raised his crystal goblet in a toast. 'I have begun to read your book on geometry, Euclid,' he said. 'I commend you for your excellent work.' Many people nodded in agreement. Euclid just bowed his head; he was always humble and quiet. Then Ptolemy turned to face Euclid and placed his hand on the mathematician's shoulder. 'But you know I am a very busy man. Running this kingdom takes a great deal of time!'" Grandfather savored the drama of the moment.

"Then Ptolemy made a bad mistake, even for a king. He asked, 'Euclid, isn't there a shorter path to mathematical understanding?'"

Alex and Theon looked at each other, pretending to be shocked.

"Can you believe it?" Grandfather shouted. "He wanted an easy way!"

Grandfather shook his head in amazement, as if the king and Euclid had just appeared before him. Then he completed the story in a quiet but firm voice.

"Euclid stood and spoke softly, with much respect. 'Your highness, I beg your pardon. We all know that throughout Egypt there are two sets of roads—one for your highness and one for the common people.' Here he raised his two arms, one for each road. 'This is as it should be. However, even for you, Sire, there is no royal road to geometry.'"

Grandfather sat back in his chair, waiting for his family to applaud as if they had never heard the story before. They obliged him. After all, it *was* a good story!

OMAR KHAYYAM (ky-AHM), ca. 1048–1131, was a Persian mathematician and astronomer, better known in the West for his poetry. His chief contribution to mathematics was the solution of cubic equations through geometry.

A Fortune Shared

"Okay, guys. Pay attention."

Nizam and Omar turned their eyes towards their friend, Hassan. He liked to be in charge, so they let him.

"Everyone knows that students of the Imam are destined to find wealth and good fortune," Hassan explained. "It is most probable that each of us will find riches before we are old."

"Sounds good to me," Nizam joked. "The sooner the better."

"But, just in case," Hassan continued without smiling, "let's make a pact. I propose that we promise to split whatever fortune comes our way. This will increase the chances for each of us. Whoever is first in accomplishing this goal will share his wealth or position or power with the other two. Agreed?"

Nizam and Omar looked at each other and shrugged their shoulders. "Why not?" they said in unison. All three were proud to be students of the Imam Mowaffak in their hometown of Naishapur. Throughout Persia, it was widely believed that his pupils had a great chance of attaining fortune. The Imam was old already, over eighty-five years old, in fact. The three friends continued to study hard to learn as much as they could from the wise teacher.

As time went by, the friends grew up and lost touch with each other.

It was Nizam who first achieved prominence. He was chosen to be vizier, or prime minister, to the sultan. In his important office, Nizam had the power to appoint others to positions of prestige. He did not forget his promise to his school friends, and sent for them one at a time.

"Omar," said Nizam, "what government post appeals to you? Perhaps you would like to be director of the observatories or minister of the arts."

Omar blushed at the offer. He knew this was a wonderful opportunity. His name, Khayyam, meant "tent-maker," and that was his family's vocation. It was an honorable profession but not very profitable. This was Omar's chance to gain wealth and power, and to become a famous man in the government.

Omar had changed, however. He no longer cared for riches or responsibility. All he really wanted was to be free to study and write.

"Thank you very much, my friend," he smiled. "Your offer is gracious and kind, but I am not suited for such a role."

"Please, Omar," Nizam protested. "There must be something I can do for you. Remember our pact as children? What would you enjoy?"

Omar Khayyam thought for a moment and cleared his throat. "There is one thing you could do. I would be most grateful, Nizam, if you could give me a little corner in which I could work. Is there a place somewhere under the shadow of your fortune where I may spread wide the advantages of science?"

Omar Khayyam's request was granted. Nizam awarded him a yearly salary with very few responsibilities. This allowed Omar time to research and write as he pleased, free from the worries of making a living.

Next, Nizam met with his other friend, Hassan. Hassan's request was not nearly as humble as Omar's. "I'd like to be the court chamberlain, Nizam. There are many legal procedures and practices I could reform if I were assigned to such a post," he boasted.

Nizam was troubled by Hassan's attitude, but Nizam would never go back on his word. He had pledged to share his good fortune with his two friends. As soon as he was able, he arranged for Hassan's appointment.

Hassan quickly became dissatisfied in his new position. His jealousy and greed caused him to plot to replace his friend Nizam. By bribing some of the other servants of the sultan with offers of wealth and position, Hassan enlisted their support. Finally, they concocted a plan to overthrow the government and take command themselves.

The sultan and Nizam, however, became aware of the rebels' sinister scheme. They dragged Hassan and his cohorts before the court, exposing their plans for the overthrow. Hassan was disgraced. Not only had he ruined his own chances for power, but he had destroyed the reputations of those who had been persuaded to follow him. He left the country with strict instructions to never return. Angry and vengeful, he skulked away from the best chance of his lifetime. In his heart, he promised himself, "Someday I will repay Nizam for this!"

For some time, no one knew where Hassan had gone nor what had happened to him. Then, suddenly, he surfaced as the leader of a violent, murderous group of fanatics. They seized a castle in the mountains south of the Caspian Sea, using it as headquarters while they terrorized the Mohammedan world. The word *assassin* may be traced to Hassan's name, or to the hashish his followers used to drug themselves into a frenzy before raiding the countryside.

One evening the steward of the court entered Omar Khayyam's workroom. "Sir, may I interrupt you a moment?" the steward asked.

"Yes, come in," Khayyam said. "What is it?"

"Bad news, sir. I'm sorry to have to tell you."

Khayyam put down what he had been reading to give the steward his full attention. "Go on. What is it?"

"It's the vizier, sir. Your friend, Nizam, has been killed by Hassan and his gang." The messenger paused while Khayyam absorbed the horrible news. "They have no respect for life or authority, sir. I'm sorry. I know this is hard for you." Omar hung his head in sadness. It took a long time for him to get over the needless death of his friend.

Some time later, Omar Khayyam was invited to work for the shah at Samarkand as a court astrologer. But Khayyam did not believe in astrology. He was an astronomer. The true science of the heavens was much more fascinating to him than what he considered to be foolish predictions. But because there was an excellent observatory in the capital city of Isfahan, Khayyam could not pass up the opportunity. He accepted the position.

"Omar," said the shah one day. "I am feeling restless and bored. Consult the stars to see what I should do."

Khayyam looked through his instruments and came back with a response. "Your highness, I see many exciting events in your future. The stars say that this is a good time for you to travel." Of course, Khayyam was only pretending to interpret the skies for the shah, who in his ignorance was pleased.

"Thank you, good man," the shah responded. "It is clear to me that you are a very wise man with good insight." He nodded his head in approval. All of his attendants nodded with him, content that the astrologer had done his duty.

One of Khayyam's scientific projects in Isfahan was the revision of the calendar. Everyone recognized at the time that the calendar they were using was inaccurate. Khayyam led a team of eight astronomers assigned to the project. By carefully observing the positions of the moon and stars, they created an impressively accurate calendar. Today, Khayyam is given credit for this amazing work.

When he wasn't observing the sun, the stars, and the planets, Omar Khayyam was studying mathematics. When he was still young, Khayyam made several original discoveries.

Khayyam believed that algebra and geometry were closely related. Many scholars in Europe and Asia disagreed with him. In his writing, Khayyam boldly declared, "No attention should be paid to the fact that algebra and geometry are different in appearance. Algebras are geometric facts that are proved."

Omar Khayyam was especially intrigued by the solution of cubic equations. He carefully and systematically classified the various kinds of cubic equations, and showed that they could be solved geometrically. Khayyam used the conic sections—circles, ellipses, parabolas, and hyperbolas. (These curves are called conic sections because they result when a plane intersects a cone.) By intersecting two conic sections, he was able to solve any cubic equation that had a positive number as a solution. Khayyam had made a remarkable discovery. It is often considered the most important advance in mathematics in the eleventh century.

Omar Khayyam was also intrigued by Euclid's postulates. In approximately 300 B.C., Euclid had published a list of postulates, mathematical statements that are accepted as true without proof. For many years, mathematicians tried to prove Euclid's fifth postulate. This postulate states that through a point not on a given line, one and only one line can be drawn parallel to the given line. If this statement could be proved, they reasoned, it would no longer be a postulate. Khayyam did not find a clear answer, but his reasoning laid the groundwork for a whole new way of doing geometry in the years to come.

Khayyam compiled his insights in a major mathematics textbook. His book has a long title but is sometimes simply called *Algebra.* In *Algebra,* he refers to another of his books, which has unfortunately been lost. There he described how he worked with the famous arithmetic triangle, which later became known as *Pascal's Triangle.*

Omar Khayyam's findings could have helped mathematicians around the world. But *Algebra,* like many works of significant Islamic mathematicians, was never translated into other languages. Thus, Khayyam's discoveries were unknown in Europe, where mathematicians were forced to rediscover many of the same truths several centuries later.

Omar Khayyam was also a poet. In fact, he is best known in the Western world as the author of the *Rubaiyat.* This collection of four-line poems is famous for its romantic, musical verse. When it was translated into English for the first time in the mid-1800s, readers throughout Europe and America were greatly impressed with the simple yet powerful poetry. It was an instant success.

Khayyam loved being outdoors where he was free to observe the beauty of nature. Sometimes he taught his students in a garden. "What a gorgeous evening this is!" Khayyam sometimes would shout, startling his students who had been concentrating deeply on a problem.

One day when the roses were especially fragrant, he stopped the lesson to speak to a student named Khwajah.

"When I die," Khayyam said, "I want to be buried near a garden. When the north wind blows, the petals from roses shall cover my tomb." Khayyam swept his arm over the scene before him. Khwajah could almost see the rose petals scattering.

Then it was back to mathematics. Years later, after Omar Khayyam had died, Khwajah remembered that quiet moment in the garden, and went to visit his teacher's grave. He found an exquisite assortment of fruit trees draping the garden wall near the tomb. The tombstone itself was covered with blossoms.

In 1884, more than 700 years after Omar Khayyam's death, an artist from England visited the tomb. He had heard of Khayyam's wish and was curious to see how the burial site would look. Although much of the area had been neglected, the artist sat down to sketch the scene. Suddenly a beautiful wild rose tree growing near the grave caught his eye. The roses were past blooming, but a few petals remained on the tombstone.

LEONARD OF PISA or **FIBONACCI** (fee-boh-NAH-chee), ca. 1180–1250, was an Italian mathematician who popularized the use of Hindu-Arabic numerals throughout Europe. He worked in algebra and geometry, and introduced the Fibonacci sequence.

Lean on the Blockhead

It was never comfortable sitting cross-legged on the floor at school, but Leonard was especially restless today. He could hear the murmuring of the crowd through the open window.

"Leonard, what is your solution to this problem?" his teacher asked.

Leonard was straining to hear what was going on outside.

"Leonard, I am speaking to you!" his teacher threatened. "Why aren't you paying attention?"

Leonard looked down at his wax tablet. Where his answer to the problem should have been, the wax was smooth. His writing instrument, a bone stylus, was upside down on his lap. He didn't even remember what the problem was!

"I'm sorry, Sir," he stammered. "I suppose I was thinking about the tower again."

It wasn't the first time Leonard had been caught daydreaming. In fact, the excitement on the streets of Pisa was distracting all the boys. Who could concentrate on geometry when there was a *real* problem to solve just outside the window?

The beautiful cathedral in Pisa had recently been completed and work had begun on the bell tower. Marble blocks had been carefully fitted into place, layer upon layer, until the tower was now three stories tall. The engineers planned for eight stories, but something had obviously gone wrong. At first the people of Pisa hoped it was just an illusion, but their hopes were soon dashed. The tower was leaning.

Everyone, even people with no building experience, had an opinion. Sometimes, Leonard's head seemed to spin as people shouted suggestions in the street.

"If you ask me, I think we should take the whole thing down and start over."

"Are you crazy? We've worked more than a year to get this far. Starting over would take forever!"

"Someone must have measured the blocks incorrectly. Why can't we get decent workers nowadays?"

Finally, the cause of the problem was determined. Because the soil in Pisa was very sandy, the foundation had settled unevenly. There was no way to correct that now, but the engineer in charge of the project had a plan.

"We'll thicken the remaining layers of blocks on the leaning side," he announced. "By the time we reach the eighth story, the tower will no longer lean. It should be perfectly straight."

The engineer's plan was carried out, but it backfired. When the extra weight was added to the leaning side, it sank even more. By the time the tower was finished two centuries later, it leaned almost seventeen feet!

Leonard was fascinated by the tower of Pisa, and had begun to understand how important it was to plan carefully. He also thought it was interesting that people had different ideas about how to solve problems. "Someday," he thought, "I hope I can be good at solving problems."

Life in Pisa was never dull, even without the tower dilemma. Leonard especially loved the life at the busy wharf, because every week ships arrived in Pisa from faraway places. Leonard's favorite pastime was to go down to the docks and watch the ships as they were loaded and unloaded. Each merchant had several employees to count cargo, and to keep careful records of receipts and expenditures. Leonard watched as their fingers flew over their abacuses. He marveled at how quickly they calculated on their boards of beads. They recorded their totals using Roman numerals, sometimes making a long row of figures in their books.

Even as a young boy, Leonard thought there must be an easier way to keep financial records. Roman numerals were okay for adding or subtracting, but impractical for multiplication and division. The abacus worked well, but it was clumsy. Besides, there was no way to check your work except to do it all over again. If you got a different answer the second time, you'd have to do it over, or get a friend to try on another abacus.

One day when Leonard was about twelve years old, his father, Bonacci, called him aside with some news.

"Leonard, you know that Pisa controls a port in Algeria, don't you?"

"Yes, Father. I think everyone knows about the customs house in Bougie."

His father paused, choosing his words carefully. "Bougie is a beautiful city, filled with people from many exotic places."

Leonard was puzzled and impatient. He wanted to get over to the pier where a ship was just docking. "What is it, Father? Why are you telling me this?"

"Leonard, I have been assigned to be the chief officer there, in Bougie, beginning immediately. It's quite a good promotion for me, and I hope it won't upset your life too much."

"What do you mean?"

"You see, I must go as soon as possible. In a short time, I will send for you. Until then, you must be strong and work hard in school."

Leonard was sorry to think of leaving Pisa and his friends. But he looked forward to the journey across the Mediterranean Sea. He had heard stories about the coast of North Africa, and he could hardly wait to see it for himself. He loved and admired his father a great deal, and he determined to make his father proud.

"Of course, Father," Leonard said bravely. "I will stay here and take care of things until you send for me. Promise me it will be soon!"

To show his loyalty to his father, Leonard chose a nickname for himself. "From now on," he announced to his friends at school, "my name will be Fibonacci, which means Son of Bonacci."

After joining his father in Algeria, young Fibonacci learned far more than he had in school. Bougie was a wealthy city, full of cultural richness and diversity. Scholars from all around the world came to share their ideas. Some were busy translating great Greek literature into Arabic. Others excitedly discussed the latest scientific discoveries.

Fibonacci stared wide-eyed at everything he saw. As he walked along the wharf, he admired the colorful costumes the sailors wore. Some of them spoke in unusual languages, and Fibonacci imagined they were telling of dangerous days on the sea.

The merchants here were using a system of bookkeeping that intrigued Fibonacci. They made strange marks on their tablets that did not resemble Roman numerals at all. Once, as he stood staring at a tablet over the shoulder of an accountant, the man began to grumble.

"What's the idea, young man? Why don't you mind your own business?"

Fibonacci hurried on his way. But after awhile, he noticed a grandfatherly man also keeping accounts, and decided to investigate.

"Excuse me, sir. May I ask you a question?" he asked timidly.

"Forty-seven, forty-eight, forty-nine . . . what? Oh bother, where was I?"

Fibonacci was afraid he would be chased off like a common wharf rat, but he stood his ground.

"I'd like to know what those marks are that you're making in your book, sir," he explained.

"What? These?" the man asked, pointing to a row of numbers. "Why, these are numbers, son, Hindu numbers. Best way to keep accounts ever invented."

After just a short lesson, Fibonacci was on his way. He whistled as he walked down the pier, proud and excited about what he had learned. Wouldn't it be great if everyone knew about the Hindu numbers?

When Fibonacci was older, he set out on his own to travel. He spent several years in Constantinople, then visited Egypt, Syria, Sicily, and Provence. Everywhere he went, he looked for other people who also were interested in numbers. Sometimes he helped them with problems, and sometimes they had answers to questions he had puzzled over for years.

Finally Fibonacci settled down in Pisa to write. His book, *Liber Abaci* (Book of the Abacus), was published in 1202. (At that time there were no printing presses. Every page of every book had to be painstakingly copied by hand.) Fibonacci was eager to see how people would respond to his ideas, particularly since he knew that some of his suggestions might be considered radical.

Fibonacci's book began this way:

> "The nine Hindu figures are: 1, 2, 3, 4, 5, 6, 7, 8, 9. With these nine figures, and with the sign 0, any number may be written."

Fibonacci proposed that Italy, and all of Europe, should use Hindu-Arabic numerals instead of Roman numerals. He cited many examples to demonstrate how much easier it was to multiply and divide using digits. At first, most people refused to consider the plan. After all, they argued, Roman numerals had worked just fine for centuries!

Some of Fibonacci's other ideas also took some getting used to. Most of his readers were not accustomed to using zero as a placeholder. He introduced a new way of writing fractions, too, placing a bar between the numerator and the denominator. Of course, since Arabs read from right to left, the fraction was on the left side of the whole number.

Fibonacci introduced a famous number sequence in his book. In this sequence each number is the sum of the two numbers preceding it. Fibonacci's sequence was the first sequence known in Europe in which the relation between two or more successive terms could be expressed by a formula. Here are the first terms in the sequence:

1, 1, 2, 3, 5, 8, 13, 21, 34, 55

Mathematicians have been intrigued by this sequence ever since Fibonacci identified it. In the 1800s, many surprising applications of the Fibonacci sequence were discovered in nature. Botanists found that the patterns of leaf buds on many stems follow the sequence, as do the spirals of seeds in the heads of sunflowers, the petals on artichokes, and the scales on pineapples. The more one looks, the more one sees them!

As a young boy, Fibonacci had chosen his own nickname. When he was older, he chose another. Sometimes he called himself "Leonardo Bigollo." The word *bigollo* has more than one meaning. It may mean *traveler*, which Fibonacci certainly was, but it may also mean *blockhead*. When skeptics wanted to ridicule his ideas, they taunted Fibonacci by calling him the *Bigollo*.

Some people think that Fibonacci especially enjoyed using this nickname as his signature on his later work. It was rewarding to show the European world what a blockhead could do! No one would laugh at Fibonacci today, though, because he is considered the greatest mathematician of the Middle Ages.

BOOK ON
GAMES
OF
CHANCE
Cardano
CARDANO
my
Life
ARS
MAGNA
CARDANO
Ars Magna Cardano

GEROLAMO CARDANO (kahr-DAH-noh), 1501–1576, was an Italian mathematician, physician, and astrologer. He advanced the development of algebra, established the use of negative and imaginary numbers, and pioneered the study of probability.

The Conceited Hypochondriac

"Thanks for the herbs, Dr. Cardano. I'll see you again next month." Knowing how the old doctor liked to talk, the young man and his friend moved quickly toward the door.

"Just a minute, my friends," exclaimed Dr. Cardano. Grabbing a book off his desk, he positioned himself between his patients and the door. "Have you seen my latest book?"

"Yes, the last time we were . . ."

"Oh, you will be very interested in this," he continued, ignoring their protests. "It's called *The Book of My Life*. See this chapter, here. It lists all the famous people in the world who have mentioned me in their writings. There are over seventy-five people in all." He paused for a quick study of their faces and smiled. "I am quite famous, you know."

The one thing Gerolamo Cardano wanted in life was fame. To be forgotten after death—that was an unbearable thought. He determined as a young teenager to do something so that future generations would recognize his name. Cardano decided to become a doctor. He would cure important people and gain lasting notoriety.

"Dr. Cardano, I just haven't been feeling strong lately," complained an elderly woman in the office one day. "Do you think there's something wrong with me?"

"Wrong with you? Hmm . . ." the old doctor mused. "Well, maybe. We'll see. By the way, have I told you about all the illnesses I've had? Look, they're right here in my autobiography in the chapter about my medical problems. You've at least felt well when you were younger, but I've always been sick. In fact, I was half dead when I was born!"

Cardano flipped through the pages until he came to the right chapter. As she listened to the self-centered doctor rehearse his list of ailments, the old woman's head began to throb. ". . . indigestion, gout, rupture, heart palpitations, hemorrhoids, insomnia, carbuncles, colic, plague, tertian fever, and poor circulation."

"You know, even when I am in the best of health I suffer from a cough and hoarseness," he whispered, clutching his throat.

"But, doctor, you have lived a long life and you've always seemed perfectly healthy to me." By saying this, the woman hoped to encourage him.

"Nonsense, woman! I could die at any minute. Very few people are ever as sick as I am," he boasted.

That night, as he rested on his couch, Cardano told his grandson Fazio about the day's patients. "Some of them had bad intentions. One can never be too careful," he warned, shaking his finger. "I'm sure several were planning to poison me, because they're jealous." He sprang to his feet and began to pace the floor.

Fazio was used to this sort of tirade; it happened almost every night. "Now, now, Grandfather. Calm down. Why would anyone want to kill you? You help your patients and they appreciate you. I'm sure this is just your imagination."

"Don't be so sure, Fazio. Some day, when you are a great man like me, you will understand. If you are successful, other people hate you."

"Tell me the story about the Archbishop in Edinburgh, Grandfather." Although Fazio knew the story like he knew his own name, he hoped it would distract Cardano from his negative thinking.

"Oh, the archbishop, yes. Well, in those days people knew greatness when they saw it and they knew how to show appreciation and respect. I was living in Milan with your grandmother and your father, God rest his soul. The College of Physicians had finally recognized me and accepted me as a member. Before long, I was the number one doctor in Italy. All over Europe, people wanted my diagnoses and cures. Why, I even treated the Pope for a minor ailment, some sort of rash on his feet, as I recall.

"Then one day I received a message—the Archbishop of Scotland was deathly ill and no one had been able to find the cause of his problem. He couldn't breathe well, you see, and everyone expected him to die soon. I had a lot of important patients, but I said I'd take a look at him and see what I could do.

"Such journeys were no laughing matter in those days," Cardano continued. "It was a long way from Milan to Edinburgh in 1552."

"It's still a long way," Fazio corrected.

"Uh, yes, of course," replied his grandfather, looking a little embarrassed. "Anyway, as I traveled across Europe, I was treated royally. So was Plato, by the way, when he traveled.

"By the time I got to Scotland I had heard many opinions about the Archbishop's case. Almost everyone thought he had a lung infection. But when I met and observed him, I came to a different conclusion. You see, because the Archbishop was tired, he spent much time in bed. But when he arose, he felt worse than before. I noticed that he slept on a fluffy feather bed with his head on an expensive leather pillow.

"Ah, ha, I thought. He is allergic. I told him to replace his feather bed with a silk bed, and to sleep on a linen pillow instead of a leather one. He did. Almost instantly, he could breathe again. Soon he began to laugh and sing, and feel more energetic.

"Don't you want to know what he gave me?" asked Cardano, expecting his grandson's usual question.

"Oh, yes," lied Fazio. "What did he give you, Grandfather?"

"The Archbishop gave me a stupendous gift—1800 gold crowns. More importantly, he awarded me letters of introduction to all of the finest people in Europe. He said that if I ever needed anything, he was ready to offer assistance."

"Is he the one who sent you to visit the King of England on your way home?"

"Now, Fazio, you know I don't like to talk about that. Would you like to go for a walk?"

Fazio knew that his grandfather was embarrassed about that visit. He had predicted that the fifteen-year-old King Edward VI would live a long but sickly life. He would die, Cardano had said, when he reached the age of fifty-five years, three months, and seventeen days. However, the king died the next year at the age of

sixteen. To cover his mistake, Cardano falsely accused the king's subjects of poisoning him.

Fazio was amazed that his elderly grandfather was wealthy and famous, considering some of his earlier escapades as a professor of mathematics. The worst incident Fazio remembered involved several other prominent mathematicians. No one knew for sure how much of the story was true, since none of the people involved had a reputation for honesty.

Cardano had been working on a book about algebra, *Ars Magna*, (*Great Art*). He and his young assistant, Ludovico Ferrari, became aware of a new discovery—a rule or formula for solving cubic equations. Mathematicians in Europe knew how to solve linear and quadratic equations. However, if an equation included a cube of a variable, such as $x^3 + px^2 = n$, they knew of no algebraic formula that would work.

Cardano and Ferrari heard that Nicolo Fontana, nicknamed Tartaglia, had discovered a formula for solving this kind of equation. They politely asked for the permission to include the rule in Cardano's book. Tartaglia refused; he wanted to reveal it himself in a book he planned to write. The two parties exchanged a series of insulting and threatening letters, with Tartaglia refusing to budge. Finally, Cardano changed his tactics. He invited Tartaglia for a visit, lavishing him with gifts and compliments. After some time, Tartaglia agreed to share his rule—cleverly encoded in a poem—on the condition that Cardano would swear to keep the secret until Tartaglia himself had printed it.

Cardano took an oath, but he regretted it. He and Ferrari built on Tartaglia's work, but they felt stifled by their inability to share it. Shouldn't the world be told of this great discovery as soon as possible? Then they heard that another mathematician, Scipiore del Ferro, had solved the same problem and, before he died, shared his secret with his student, Antonio Fior. Fior eventually yielded to the flattery of Cardano and showed him the rule. Since someone else had also solved the problem, Cardano felt his promise to Tartaglia was void. He quickly published *Ars Magna,* including Tartaglia's secret. Although he gave Tartaglia credit for the discovery, Tartaglia was outraged.

Later in his life, Cardano often pointed to his autobiography when the subject of Tartaglia came up. "Look here," he would say to a visitor. "This is all I have to say on the subject." The visitor would read Cardano's words. *I have never . . . divulged the secrets of my former friends*. The secret rule, borrowed from Tartaglia, came to be known as *Cardano's Formula*. It opened new areas of equations for exploration and study.

Although Cardano worked as a mathematician and a physician—sometimes simultaneously—he always made time to write. Though he claimed to be sick, he had incredible energy. During his lifetime, he wrote over 7000 pages on a wide range of topics. At least 131 of his works were published, and another 111 were found in manuscript form when he died. He claimed to have burned 170 others.

Cardano also found time for his favorite hobby—gambling, which he claimed to have begun to provide for his wife and children. But even when he became wealthy, he continued to gamble almost every day. Out of this involvement came an exciting work, *Book on Games of Chance*. In it, Cardano provided the first systematic attempt to make probability calculations. He was the first to understand the basic notions of probability, the branch of mathematics that deals with predicting the likelihood of events. None of his contemporaries recognized its values, and his ideas were essentially forgotten until Pascal and Fermat introduced the field of probability approximately 100 years later.

In his personal life, the superstitious Cardano did not use probability to explain events. He believed he had a guardian angel who had protected him from chunks of falling masonry and saved him from shipwreck.

Fazio knew that his grandfather, Cardano, interpreted almost everything as a sign. If he heard a dog howl or a rooster crow, or saw sparks in a fire, something strange was sure to happen soon. Every knock or thump had meaning.

"Fazio! Come quickly! There it goes again. Do you hear it?"

"Hear what, Grandfather?"

"Why, that infernal buzzing, of course! Inside my left ear!" Cardano explained. "I know someone somewhere is saying something bad about me. If only my *right* ear would buzz. Then I would know someone was praising me!"

"Perhaps it's just a headache, Grandfather. Why don't you rest for awhile?"

Were it not for his grandson, Fazio, Cardano would have had no family to care for him. He was pleased when Fazio agreed to live with him, and the two became friends.

Fazio could see right through his grandfather, but he also knew that Cardano was a brilliant man who deserved respect and admiration. He was the first mathematician to understand and describe negative numbers, the first to recognize the existence of negative roots, and the first to take note of imaginary numbers. Perhaps if his situation had been different, Cardano would have been a kinder and more pleasant person.

"You know, Fazio," Cardano said one day. "I may have been wrong about the King of England, but there are some dates that my astrological calculations guarantee. I am absolutely positive that I will die on September 20, 1576, four days before my seventy-fifth birthday."

"Now, Grandfather, please don't talk like that. You're healthy and strong and are likely to live much longer than that. Besides, there are many things you need to write about."

"Don't argue with me, Fazio," Cardano scolded. "Just promise me that after my death you will publish the fact that I was correct in my prediction. I want everyone to know that I am an impeccable astrologer. My reputation must be permanently established. Do you promise?"

Fazio promised, just to ease his Grandfather's agitation. After all, family tradition didn't exactly require *keeping* promises.

On September 20, 1576, Cardano was disappointed to find himself in perfect health. No huge stone fell on him, and no great sea monster swallowed him up. In the evening, to ensure that his final prediction would be correct, he drank a glass of poison.

RENÉ DESCARTES (day-KART), 1596–1650, was a French philosopher, mathematician, and scientist. He was the co-founder of analytic geometry. By combining the study of algebra and geometry, Descartes opened a new world of mathematical possibilities.

The Stay-in-Bed Scholar

It was still dark in the dormitory when the old bell clanged and clattered, waking the boys for morning prayers. They moaned and stretched, rubbing their eyes as their feet hit the cold floor.

"It's bad enough our having to get up, but watching *him* snuggle down for another hour or two makes me angry!" Henri complained to whomever would listen.

"Makes me angry, too," chimed Jacques, hurling his pillow onto the bed of the offending snorer.

"Careful, guys," warned Emile. "Remember what Father Charlet said. 'Anyone caught harassing René Descartes in the early morning hours will be required to get up *before* the bell.'"

"Yeah, I heard him," said Jacques. "But maybe if the boy got more exercise he wouldn't be so scrawny. I don't see how spending so much time in bed is going to help him."

The three boys dressed quickly, then hurried to chapel and breakfast before beginning a full morning of classes.

Meanwhile, René Descartes sleepily opened his eyes in the sun-filled room at La Fleche school. He was almost nine years old, and this was his first year at La Fleche. He liked the school, just as his father had promised he would. He had not counted on Father Charlet, however. Father Charlet, the director of the school, liked René from the first day, and seemed to consider his physical weakness a personal challenge. As a child, René had been sick a lot. He wasn't as strong or muscular as other boys his age, but he didn't expect special privileges because of that. He suspected that the director, who seemed very kind, was experimenting with him to test a theory. Father Charlet thought staying in bed would make weak people stronger.

Except for its making other boys pick on him, lying in bed suited René just fine. He didn't sleep much. In fact, he was often awake before the bell rang, only pretending to sleep so the others wouldn't bother him. Most of the time he was thinking. The hall was quiet in the mornings, and he could concentrate on all sorts of ideas. Sometimes he figured out answers to problems from his afternoon classes. On other mornings, he made up verses or thought about topics to discuss at dinner.

During his first five years at school, Descartes studied grammar and literature. Then he devoted three years to science, philosophy, and theology, favoring mathematics above all else. He was an excellent student and took his classes seriously, but he refused to rise in the morning until he was ready. Formal study had to take place later in the day. Father Charlet had unwittingly launched Descartes' lifelong habit of staying in bed until noon—or later.

Although Descartes graduated with a law degree from the University of Poitiers, practicing law did not appeal to him. In fact, he was not at all interested in settling down with a regular job. He wanted to see the world. Like many other young men, he thought joining the army would be a good way to do this.

In the army, Descartes spent several years traveling, observing the customs and cultures of other people. Fortunately for him, there were no actual battles or wars, but long periods of leisure during which he read a lot, pondered many ideas, and began to write.

Some of Descartes' fellow soldiers questioned his behavior.

"René, why did you join the army, anyway?" Claude wondered aloud. "All you do is read books!"

"Yeah," added Albert. "You could at least lift your head and say something once in a while. Wouldn't you like a good conversation every so often?"

"As a matter of fact," Descartes answered, "I was just thinking that reading good books is like talking with great people of past times."

"Then you won't go with us to the party tonight?" Albert asked.

"Thanks anyway," Descartes replied. "I'm tired. I'll just finish this section and go to bed early. You fellows have a good time for me!"

Claude and Albert returned to camp late and went to bed quietly without disturbing Descartes. Perched on their bunks the next morning, they were eager to tell him about the girls they had met. Descartes, however, just gazed into space as they talked, rubbing his eyes and inhaling deeply. They could see that something was wrong.

"Are you sick, René?" Albert asked.

"What's wrong with you, friend? Didn't you sleep?" asked Claude.

"Claude, Albert, listen to me," Descartes began. "I have had the strangest dream!"

"Oh, so that's it," Claude laughed, poking Albert in the ribs with his elbow. "Was she pretty?"

Descartes did not even smile. He stood to his feet and began describing his dream. "There were three sections to my dream. What I saw was wonderful! I can't find the words to describe it fully, but this dream—this dream has clarified my purpose in life." He flung his arms outward as if making an announcement. "Now I know what I will do!"

"Tell us more!" begged Albert. "What happened? What did you see?"

"You probably won't understand it, Albert," replied Descartes. "But I saw the key to the secrets of nature. Everything in nature—in all of the sciences—everything is connected by mathematical links!"

Claude was thoroughly confused—and a little frightened by Descartes' excitement. "I think I'd better be going. I've got a lot of work to do," he muttered as he picked up his boots.

"Me, too," said Albert. "I'll come along with you."

Descartes immediately recorded his dream in his journal because he wanted to remember as much of it as possible. He wrote that the dream had provided a "wonderful discovery," that he had seen open books and read poetry, and that he was searching for what it all meant.

Many people think that this dream gave Descartes the idea of analytic geometry, which is the connection between algebra and geometry. Also known as coordinate geometry, it is Descartes' most important contribution to mathematics. It completely changed the way people thought about mathematics, making exciting achievements in mathematics and science possible.

The idea of analytic geometry may have come through a dream, but Descartes' habit of lounging in bed contributed to its development. One day while Descartes was resting, a pesky fly landed on the ceiling above him. The buzzing of the fly distracted him; he couldn't concentrate on the passage of poetry he was trying to memorize.

The fly was lazily crawling back and forth on the ceiling near one corner of the room. Descartes began to wonder how the position of the fly could be described. He reasoned that if one knew the distance of the fly from the two adjacent walls, its position on the ceiling could be precisely expressed. By identifying the point of the fly's position as coordinates, one could describe its path algebraically. A tiny insect had prompted a giant discovery!

After Descartes left the army, he spent several years visiting scientists and philosophers throughout western Europe. He believed that one could learn a lot from observing different cultures and situations. He kept a journal during his travels, writing down interesting facts and details to use later in his writing.

Occasionally Descartes' adventures were not exactly pleasurable. Once he engaged a small boat to take him to one of the Frisian islands. He must have made quite an impression when he arrived for the voyage dressed in a taffeta cloak and an ostrich-plumed hat. The cutthroat crew looked Descartes over and decided he was an easy target. They were sure he could not understand their language, so they foolishly plotted and schemed right in front of him.

"Okay, you sea dogs," bellowed one of the mates in charge. "Here's what we'll do. When we get far enough out to sea, away from this port, I'll get his attention, and you clobber him with that club. Then we'll strip him of these fine-looking clothes, snatch his gold, and toss him overboard."

"Good plan," echoed his shipmates. "No one will ever know what happened," they laughed, "and he won't know what hit him!"

Descartes, however, understood every word. He waited until the boat was some distance from shore. Then, before the villains had a chance to act, he whipped out his gleaming sword and caught them off guard. Holding the tip of his sword on the neck of the ring-leader, Descartes ordered the sailors to return him to shore.

Perhaps Descartes was ready for a quieter life. He eventually chose to settle in Holland, where, in seclusion, he was free to concentrate on his studies and writing. His most important book, *Discourse on Method,* is considered a landmark in the history of philosophy. Published in 1637, this book was an important catalyst for the scientific revolution of the seventeenth century.

An appendix to *Discourse* was entitled *Geometry,* the most important of Descartes' mathematical writing. In it he introduced and explained his ideas on "the marriage of algebra and geometry," and also established some new mathematical practices. For example, he used the first letters of the alphabet, a, b, and c, to denote known quantities. Unknown quantities were identified by x, y, and z. This is a custom that is still used today.

One day Descartes received a special message from Queen Christina of Sweden. She wanted him to come to Sweden to be her special tutor and advisor. She knew he had an exceptional mind, having made important contributions to physics, chemistry, physiology, and psychology, and especially to philosophy and mathematics. Almost every subject had been touched by his creative genius. "I want to build a school of sciences that will become the best in Europe," she said in her message, "and I need your help."

Descartes was flattered, but he loved his quiet home in Holland, where he stayed in bed every morning until he felt like getting up. He also enjoyed puttering around in his little garden. All of this would have to change if he accepted Christina's offer. "Why should I go live in the land of bears amongst rocks and ice?" he asked his friends. Descartes courteously declined the invitation.

Queen Christina was only nineteen years old, and not used to being refused. An expert horsewoman and huntress, she was not about to let this highly prized "prey" escape. She dispatched an admiral to persuade Descartes to change his mind. Then she sent a Swedish warship to pick him up and deliver him to her estate. Descartes found it impossible to refuse.

His fears about the cold weather were justified. When Descartes arrived in Sweden in 1649, the country was in the grip of an unusually severe winter. The cold didn't bother the hearty Christina. She was determined to study philosophy with Descartes in her frigid library with the windows open—at five o'clock in the morning. This was especially painful for a man who had enjoyed the lifelong habit of lazy mornings spent in a warm bed. But Christina was insensitive to Descartes' needs.

Descartes often regretted leaving the solitude and serenity of his home in Holland. Even the praise and admiration of the Swedish people could not make up for Christina's whimsical ways. Soon, the cold weather and the rigorous schedule took their toll on Descartes. He caught pneumonia and never recovered. He died on February 11, 1650, and was buried in a small Catholic cemetery in Stockholm.

Seventeen years later, the French government arranged to move Descartes' body to Paris. He was re-entombed in what is now the

Pantheon—at least most of him was. The French Treasurer-General, who was in charge of moving the remains, kept the bones of Descartes' right hand as a souvenir!

Most people prefer not to collect skeletal parts, even from someone famous. A lock of hair or a signature is usually enough of a souvenir. It's good to remember that the most important parts of people—their ideas and accomplishments—belong to everyone.

PIERRE DE FERMAT (fair-MAH), 1601–1685, was a French lawyer who pursued mathematics as a hobby. He is the founder of modern number theory and contributed to the development of analytic geometry, calculus, and probability. He is most famous for his last theorem, scribbled in the margin of a book.

An Amateur Becomes a Prince

"Pierre, are you coming to bed soon?"

"Yes, Louise. In a few minutes."

"Well, I hope so. I don't see how you can stay up so late and still be fresh and alert in court in the morning."

"Yes, yes. I know. But these ideas of Diophantus are quite something. I don't remember when I've read anything so delightful and challenging. And I'm really not a bit sleepy."

"If you were a mathematician I could understand it," his wife replied. "But to be so consumed by a *hobby* just doesn't make sense."

"If it's any comfort to you, dear, remember that I have been winning all my cases recently. I have never missed a court date, and my friends still enjoy my company. Surely this hobby is not harmful to me. In fact, I think I'm sharper in court because of my study of mathematics."

Louise gave up, ending the discussion as she usually did by pulling the covers up to her neck and trying to fall asleep. She knew that her husband was right about one thing. Everyone in the legal profession respected and admired him. His knowledge of the law was impressive, and he could be counted on to use it with integrity.

Fermat's mother, who had taught him at home for many years, came from a large family of jurists. It seemed natural that he would follow in their footsteps. Louise was a distant cousin of her husband's mother, and proud of his good reputation.

Right in the middle of a wonderful, soothing dream about her garden, Louise was startled awake by a loud crash.

"I've got it!" shouted Fermat, as he bent to pick up the chair he had knocked over in his excitement. "I've found a marvelous proof!" He wrote brief notes in the margin of the book, then put out the candle and sighed contentedly as he crawled into bed.

Louise also sighed, then covered her head with the pillow.

In the morning, Louise glanced at her husband's book, which lay open beside the bed. It was Diophantus' *Arithmetica*, translated into Latin by Bachet. The problem Diophantus posed was this:

> "Assuming that x, y, z, and n are positive integers, when does $x^n + y^n = z^n$ have a solution?"

Diophantus proved that when $n = 1$ and when $n = 2$ there are many solutions. But he had not been able to find a solution for $n = 3$, nor could he prove that a solution was impossible.

Louise smiled as she read Fermat's note scribbled in the margin. "I have found a truly wonderful proof that there is no solution to this problem when n is greater than 2, but the margin is too small to hold it." Thank goodness for narrow margins, she thought. Otherwise the man would never go to bed!

Fermat's tantalizing note has resulted in many a sleepless night for many a mathematician. For more than 350 years, mathematicians around the world have been trying to prove what is now known as "Fermat's Last Theorem." Hundreds of prizes have been offered for a valid proof. In 1908, 100,000 German marcs were offered to whomever could find a solution. During the next four years, more than 1000 alleged proofs were submitted, but the prize went unclaimed. Every entry was incorrect.

In 1993, a Princeton University mathematics professor, Andrew Wiles, announced that he had solved Fermat's Last Theorem. His proof, more than 200 pages long, is so complex, it may take mathematicians several years to determine its validity.

Fermat claimed to have found a remarkable proof that the equation has no solution when n is greater than 2. Since he was not in the habit of showing his work, no one is sure if he found the proof. But Fermat has an excellent record. Every other proof he claimed to have found has been proven.

Fermat always made a clear distinction between *guessing* and *proving*. In his correspondence and even in his private notes, he carefully identified what was mere conjecture and what had been mathematically proven. Because of his meticulous attention to this distinction, many scholars think he actually had found a proof. Unlike his wife Louise, they wish the margins in the book would have been a little larger.

"Pierre, why are you so stubbornly opposed to publishing your work?" his friend Roberval complained one day in the Fermat library. "I would be happy to help you. Think of how famous you'd be!"

"Why do I need to be famous?" Fermat responded. "I have everything I want—a fine position as a lawyer in parliament, a lovely family and home, and a hobby that helps me to relax. My mathematical ideas, whatever their merit, would require much polishing if I were to try to publish them. It would be a waste of time!"

Because Fermat was too modest to be attracted by glory and too content to be attracted by money, Roberval knew that he would have to try a different approach. "Think of how you could help humanity," he suggested. "You may be able to assist mathematicians in finding breakthroughs in their research."

Fermat chuckled in response. "Roberval, do you *really* think I know anything that valuable? I do this mostly for fun, you know. This fooling with numbers is quite impractical. Besides, I'm only an amateur, so let's leave publishing to the professionals."

When Fermat saw Roberval's downcast look, he took a deep breath and began again more softly. "Thank you for your good counsel, my friend. You should know that I do maintain an active correspondence with several mathematicians. I will help them whenever and however I can. In fact, I am working with Pascal right now on some predictions of chance. Tonight, however, I would like to finish reading this wonderful play by Sophocles."

Only one of Fermat's manuscripts was published during his lifetime, and it was published anonymously, signed with fictitious initials. But some of the mathematicians he corresponded with kept his letters. These letters reveal a lot about Fermat's personality and about his mathematical achievement.

In the summer of 1654, Fermat exchanged a series of letters with Pascal, whom he never met in person. Both of them had contemplated the theory of probability. They began collaborating, doing experiments and comparing results. Many of these studies pointed to similar conclusions. Both Fermat and Pascal were pleased.

Fermat wrote one letter specifically to affirm Pascal's work in probability.

> Toulouse, August 29, 1654
>
> Sir,
>
> Our double thrusts still keep up, and like you I am struck with admiration that our ideas fit so perfectly it seems as if they have taken the same road and covered the same distance. . . . I am not afraid of going astray as long as I fall in with you in this way, and I am convinced that the true method of avoiding error is to find oneself in agreement with you.
>
> Fermat

Fermat often spoke of his opinions of algebra and geometry. "Algebra is a wonderful gift to mankind," he proclaimed. "Its many rules and formulas can become confusing, however. Geometry, on the other hand, shows us much about the real world. Still, it can become too abstract."

Since neither algebra nor geometry was perfect, Fermat thought of a plan. If one borrowed the best ideas from algebra and the best approaches from geometry, perhaps the weaknesses of each could be overcome with the help of the other. This led to Fermat's development of analytic geometry, which occurred about the same time as Descartes' work on the subject.

Fermat and Descartes did not correspond with each other until much later. Neither knew about the other's accomplishments, yet their conclusions were amazingly similar. The temperamental Descartes was a little suspicious of Fermat's work. Fermat, on the other hand, was delighted to find that a prestigious mathematician and philosopher agreed with an amateur like himself.

Although Fermat made important contributions to probability theory and analytic geometry, his favorite pastime was what is now called number theory. He loved to look for patterns and relationships among whole numbers. One evening while relaxing after a day at the office, he began thinking about prime numbers—numbers that are divisible only by themselves and one. Except for the number 2, all prime numbers are odd. Fermat thought about the odd primes—3, 5, 7, 11, 13, 17, and so on. He noticed that certain primes could be expressed as the sum of two square numbers. For example, $5 = 1 + 4$, $13 = 4 + 9$, and $17 = 1 + 16$.

Some primes, however, could not be expressed this way. He began to wonder. When can an odd prime be expressed as the sum of two squares?

After much trial and error, he found the key. Divide the prime by 4 and look at the remainder. If the remainder is 1, the prime may be expressed as the sum of the two squares. If the remainder is 3, it cannot be done. Fermat knew that dividing an odd prime by 4 will always leave a remainder of either 1 or 3.

As usual, Fermat did not write a neat, thorough proof of this theorem. In fact, it wasn't proven for over 100 years. Euler labored seven years to find a proof, and finally succeeded in 1749. Known as the *Two-Square Theorem,* this is considered one of the most beautiful of Fermat's discoveries.

Perhaps it seems unusual to think of a mathematical discovery as beautiful. For Fermat, that's just what it was. He found as much elegance and harmony in mathematics as others find in music or painting. Thinking about mathematics refreshed him in the same way listening to a symphony might rejuvenate someone else.

Nothing in Fermat's childhood nourished his interest in mathematics. His father was a leather merchant, not a famous mathematician. Nor was Fermat a child prodigy. In fact, he did not receive a formal education in mathematics beyond the most elementary levels. His life was not dedicated to solving famous problems and he was not interested in publishing his work. He was, however, passionately interested in the subject and devoted much of his spare time to it. In spite of all this, he is recognized as one of the greatest French mathematicians of the seventeenth century. Scholars and historians have bestowed on him a royal title, The Prince of Amateurs.

Agnesi
Foundations of Analysis
AGNESI

MARIA AGNESI (ah NYA zi), 1718–1799, is the most celebrated Italian woman of the scientific revolution. Her calculus textbook, *Foundations of Analysis*, is the most important publication in mathematics by a woman up to that time.

The Gift of Simplicity

Bong . . . bong, struck the parlor clock. Maria scowled at the calculus problem staring up at her from her desk. It was two A.M., and she knew she needed her rest. Without it, she would be too tired to make her rounds at the hospital in the morning. Maria made a face at the paper on her desk. She had been working on this infuriating problem since dinner, and everything she tried led to a dead end.

Maria heard her sisters' quiet breathing in the peaceful night. Finally, she abandoned her work at the desk and crawled into bed beside them. The problem would have to wait until the next day.

In the morning, Maria felt the warmth of bright sunlight shining through the shutters. She stretched and yawned, wondering where the night had gone, then dragged herself out of bed and over to her desk. "*That's* why I'm so tired," she remembered, glancing at the calculations covering the sheet of papers. "That problem kept me up until two!" She determined to rethink the problem before breakfast, but before her pen had touched the paper, she froze.

"Teresa!" she gasped. "Did you do this?"

Teresa moaned and pulled the blankets over her head. "Do what?"

Maria was speechless. She knew she had gone to bed in frustration with the problem unsolved. But there, before her on her desk, was the solution in her own neat handwriting. Was she dreaming?

Teresa sat up in bed. "Why can't you have pity on us and let us get some sleep, Maria?" she growled. "It's bad enough that you do mathematics every spare minute of your day! Why do you have to get up in the middle of the night like that?"

"What do you mean 'middle of the night'?" asked Maria.

"What would you call 3:30 A.M.?" yawned Teresa. "I couldn't believe it when I heard you get up, light the lantern, and sit down at your desk. Don't you ever get tired of that stuff?"

Maria rubbed her eyes and looked at the problem again. The night before, she never would have thought of solving the problem that way. But there was no denying what had happened. Although she couldn't remember doing it, she had solved the problem in her sleep!

After that, Maria Agnesi gained quite a reputation as a somnambulist. She frequently walked and worked in her sleep, much to the amusement—and sometimes annoyance—of her family and friends.

Maria's family knew from her childhood that she was especially gifted. At the age of five, she learned to speak French fluently. Four years later, she could speak Latin, Hebrew, and Greek. Her excellent memory seemed to make learning a game.

Throughout Europe, Latin was the most important language for scholars; most of the great philosophers wrote in Latin. Maria demonstrated how skilled she was in Latin when a proposal she wrote on the importance of higher education for women was published. She was only *nine years old* at the time.

Maria's parents were so proud of her remarkable skill in philosophy and mathematics that her father hired some of the best tutors in Italy to teach her. When Maria was a teenager, he was ready to show her off. He invited his intellectual friends to a series of Friday night discussions, and asked Maria to demonstrate her abilities.

At first, she enjoyed being tested and challenged on abstract mathematical questions and complex philosophical ideas. It certainly wasn't something she could do with her girl friends. But after awhile, it became tiresome. Too often there was someone in the group who wanted to embarrass her—to find something she might not know.

Her displeasure came to a head one particular Friday evening, when the Crown Prince of Saxony was in attendance. He sat up straight as an arrow, cleared his throat, and adjusted his collar.

"Excuse me, Miss Agnesi," he began in a strong voice. "Have you read Descartes' *Rules for the Direction of the Mind*?"

"Yes, sir, I have."

"In French?"

"Yes, sir, in French." Maria Agnesi wondered where this question was leading. They had been talking about Descartes' geometry, not his philosophy.

Tension suddenly filled the room. Had the prince found a discrepancy in Maria's reasoning? Everyone grew quiet as they waited for the usually somber prince to continue.

All at once, he slapped his knee and burst into laughter. "Well," he blurted, "I think you could have *written* it!"

Everyone laughed with relief, except Maria. She was tired of being on display for her father's friends like some sort of intellectual freak. The next morning, Maria approached her father who was reading in his library. "May I come in, Father?" she asked softly.

"Of course, Maria. What is it?"

"I admire you very much, Father. You know that, don't you?"

"Why, yes. I believe I do."

"And you know that I have always appreciated your work as a mathematician and professor," she continued quietly. "You have given me every advantage in education and have always encouraged me to develop my interests and abilities. For that I can never thank you enough."

"You're welcome, Maria," he replied smiling, about to turn back to his work.

"Father," she hesitated. "I would like to be excused from the Friday sessions from now on."

"You *what*?" gasped her father.

Now that the truth was out, Maria quickly unleashed all her arguments. "Teresa enjoys playing her harpsichord on these evenings, and she can continue. The gentlemen will surely be able to carry on their discussions without me—they are so learned and well-read, you know."

"But, . . ." said her father, trying to get a word in.

"I don't mean to be disrespectful, Father, but I have been doing this for you for five years now, and I believe it is time for me to follow my heart, instead of only my mind."

She breathed deeply, trying to stay calm as her father sorted through his thoughts.

"What's come over you, Maria?" he pleaded. "Don't you know how fortunate we are to be visited by the most brilliant men in Italy? And not just Italy. Why, they come from all around Europe to hear you. Your sister may play the harpsichord well, but you know they don't come for that." He shook his head in frustration. "Follow your heart? That's nonsense. Leave me alone now. We'll talk again when you have had time to think about what you are saying!"

Maria left silently, her heart pounding from the confrontation with her father. She truly did not want to hurt him, but she had other plans for her life.

Finally, she gathered the courage to speak to her father again. "Father," she announced. "I have decided to become a nun and move to the convent. I would like to help the sick and the poor rather than entertain the wealthy and the educated."

"Maria," he said quietly, "I must forbid this. I'm sorry, but I must."

He took her hand and gently led her to a chair. "We will make a bargain. You need not come to our *conversaziones* on Friday evenings, but please don't go to the convent. If you stay home, I will grant you whatever else you wish."

Maria was disappointed, but her heart was warmed by her father's loving tone. She made three requests, which her father quickly granted. First, she asked to be allowed to dress simply and modestly, almost as if she were living in a convent. Secondly, she requested the privilege of attending church whenever she liked. Last, she begged to be excused from attending balls, the theater, and other such social occasions. They both seemed satisfied with the agreement.

One of Maria's responsibilities at home was teaching mathematics to her younger brothers. When she became dissatisfied with the available textbooks, she began to write her own explanations and to design worksheets to help them understand the subject. When she learned that other students needed help too, she decided to compile her work into a book.

Whenever she found time, Maria worked on her project. Over a period of ten years, she composed a systematic presentation of algebra, analytic geometry, calculus, and differential equations. She used many examples and sample problems as a teaching method to help readers better understand the concepts.

In 1748, Maria Agnesi's book, *Foundations of Analysis,* was finally ready to be published. The printer moved his equipment into her house, so that she could supervise the book's production and answer questions about details. *Foundations of Analysis,* two volumes—1070 pages on handmade paper, was widely praised by mathematicians. Teachers and scholars were thrilled to use a book so comprehensive and clear. Though written by a shy, unassuming person, it was considered the authoritative text in mathematics for fifty years.

Acclaim came to Agnesi from around the world, including the most prestigious mathematics association in the world, the French Academy of Sciences. Her book was dedicated to Empress Maria Theresa of Austria, who sent Maria a beautiful diamond ring and a small crystal box embedded with jewels. The Bologna Academy of Sciences in Italy admitted Agnesi into its membership.

But the tribute most treasured by Agnesi were the letters she received from Pope Benedict XIV. He was interested in mathematics, and personally corresponded with her about her work. He sent her a gold wreath, set with precious stones, and a gold medal marking her achievement. In 1750, upon the Pope's recommendation, she was listed at the University of Bologna as an honorary lecturer.

Agnesi's book was written in Italian and translated into several other languages. It was the English translation by John Colson, professor at Cambridge University, that resulted in the misleading "witch" stories.

One of the most brilliant sections of Agnesi's work concerns a special bell-shaped curve. This curve was called *la versiera* in Italian, an expression derived from the Latin word for *to turn*. But *versiera* was also the abbreviation for the Italian expression *avversiera*, meaning "wife of the devil" or "female goblin." Colson, who had learned Italian just so he could translate Agnesi's book, mistakenly called her famous curve the *witch curve*. Soon the curve became known throughout the English-speaking world as *the witch of Agnesi.*

Obviously, the use of the word *witch* with Maria Agnesi's name is shockingly out of place. Although she made a tremendous contribution to mathematics, Agnesi worked and wrote as a mathematician for only about twenty years. Most of her life was spent helping the poor and needy. Charity work satisfied her; she chose to live simply and quietly, giving her time and property to those less fortunate. She even sold the jewels given her by the Empress and the Pope, and gave the money to the poor. At one point, she gave up her own room to make space for several homeless women.

Once, in 1762, officials from the University of Turin wrote Agnesi a letter. "We would very much appreciate your opinion of the enclosed work of a promising young mathematician, Joseph Lagrange," the letter began. "We know of no one more capable of judging the worth and potential of this work."

Maria responded simply but firmly, "Such matters no longer occupy my mind."

Maria Agnesi, loved by many as an angel of consolation, died at the age of eighty-one on January 9, 1799. At her request, she was buried in a common grave with fifteen former residents of the home for the elderly where she had worked. No monument marks the site.

On the 100th anniversary of Agnesi's death, however, the city of Milan renamed several streets in her honor. A school in Milan bears her name, and Maria Agnesi scholarships are given annually to needy girls in the city.

Maria Agnesi's most important contribution to mathematics was her calculus textbook. The French Academy proclaimed, "There is no other book, in any language, that would enable a reader to penetrate as deeply, or as rapidly, into the fundamental concepts of analysis."

Judging by her life of service, Agnesi believed that helping others is the truly important goal of life. She left her pursuit of mathematics to become a humble servant to the poor. Perhaps even she did not realize that her contributions in both areas would make a lasting imprint on our lives. There are many ways to help others, and mathematicians can do it, too.

BENJAMIN BANNEKER, 1731–1806, was an African-American mathematician and scientist. He is best known as a compiler of almanacs and as an assistant in the surveying of the boundaries for the District of Columbia.

The Shy Sky Watcher

Benjamin flopped down on the shady grass and stretched his arms and legs as far as they would reach. He took a deep breath, inhaling the sweet orange blossom fragrance. Baltimore County, Maryland was beautiful in the early spring. Pear blossoms scattered in the breeze like snowflakes. As he gazed at the puffy white clouds in the sky, he thought, "That one moves so quickly past the sun. I wonder how fast it's traveling. But that other one, shaped like an old pipe, doesn't look like it's moving at all."

"Benjamin, Benjamin, Benjamin," teased his mother as she came trudging over the ridge. "Can't you hear me calling you? If you don't get those cows penned up, you won't get to go fishing with your father. Seems to me a boy of nine would figure that out. Now, hurry up!"

Scrambling to his feet, Benjamin murmured an apology, and tried to tell her about the clouds he was observing. His mother knew better than to wait for an explanation. Her son was always looking up. She once jokingly threatened to make him a neck collar to help tilt his head toward the sky. "Might as well save your muscles," she'd groaned.

Benjamin obediently went back to work coaxing the slowest of their three cows. "Come on, Mol. Get a move on."

His mother, still within hearing distance, stopped in her tracks. "What did you call her?"

"Mol. Short for Molly," Benjamin explained.

"That's what I thought you said. How dare you name a cow after your grandmother? What if she should hear you? What would she think of such disrespect?"

"Well, I think she would be happy, because she's the one who suggested the name."

"She did? Your grandmother told you to name a cow after her?"

Benjamin grinned and patted the cow as she lumbered into the makeshift pen. It was his job to move the cows twice a day to keep the fields evenly grazed and fertilized. He fastened the fence gate with an old rope, and continued his explanation.

"Last week when I went to visit Grandmother Molly, I told her about this cow. You know, how she's faithful and productive, but just plain stubborn about some things. Grandmother laughed and said 'Sounds like me. Why don't you call her Mol?'"

Benjamin worked hard on his family's farm. When he wasn't cowpenning, he was tending the vegetables in the garden or the fruit trees in the family's small orchard. Sometimes, his father let him help with the bees. Benjamin and his sisters were proud to have their own supply of honey right there on the farm.

In early spring it was time to plant tobacco. When the weather was still nippy, Benjamin's father would carefully plant tiny tobacco seeds from the previous year's crop in a specially prepared seedbed. Early every day, Benjamin would run to the seedbed to look for sprouts. He counted every tiny blade of green, then hurried back to the house for breakfast, where he would announce the day's total.

After several months, the seedlings were big enough for replanting, three feet apart in parallel rows. Benjamin's father knew precisely when to do this, according to the weather and the moistness of the soil. But the hard work was just beginning. Everyone in the family had to help, tramping down those rows over and over again as they pulled weeds from the ground and removed thousands of insects and worms from the plants by hand. Then each plant had to be topped, or cut back, to make it bushy and strong.

One night after a hard day's work, Benjamin wondered aloud if maybe the family should switch to beekeeping instead of tobacco. "You know," he said, "tobacco is the most troublesome plant God ever created. Today while I was hoeing, I counted thirty-six separate steps in the cultivation of tobacco."

"Benjamin," said his father sternly, "you would be wise to keep your mind on your work and quit counting. Nothing worth having in life comes easily."

Benjamin often became tired during the harvest. To keep his spirits up, he thought about the coming winter—and school. During the coldest months of the year, a small country school opened for neighborhood children. It was only a one-room school with seven or eight students, but Benjamin loved going. His grandmother Molly had taught him to read and write when he was very young, but he had no books. At school, he read everything, regardless of the subject.

When Benjamin was old enough to work all day on the farm, he had to quit school. But that didn't mean he had to quit learning. Rather than leave his beloved books behind, he borrowed them—especially mathematics books—from his former teacher and kept studying and learning on his own.

In the early 1700s most African-Americans were slaves, but the Banneker family was free. Benjamin's grandmother, Molly Welsh, had come to Maryland from England in 1683. She was an indentured servant who had to work seven years without pay for her freedom. But she was a strong and determined woman, and soon after obtaining her freedom she was able to purchase some land of her own. Although she was opposed to slavery, she knew she would need help to farm the land. The only way to get help in those days was to purchase slaves. She bought two, but quickly gave them their freedom. One of them, Bannaka, was actually the son of an African chieftain. Later, he and Molly were married, establishing the Banneker family in America.

Grandmother Molly was a powerful force in her family. She taught her children and grandchildren to read and write, to work hard, and to value independence and freedom. Benjamin's ability to remember and understand almost everything she told him made his visits to her farm some of her most treasured moments.

When Benjamin Banneker was only twenty-two years old, he did something that would have amazed even his grandmother. He built a clock. It would be difficult for anyone without training to build one, but Banneker did so after only examining the inside of a borrowed pocket watch. After sketching the gears and wheels, Banneker calculated how large they would each need to be to make the clock keep accurate time. Then he painstakingly carved the pieces from wood and fit them all together. When he was finished, the clock reported the hour, minute, and second. It even struck a gong every hour on the hour! People came from throughout the neighboring valleys to see and admire his remarkable achievement.

When his father died, Benjamin accepted responsibility for the farm, including providing for his mother and sisters. This left little time for studying or building inventions. One by one his three sisters married and left home to settle nearby. Banneker, however, was more at home in the garden or tending his bees than with other people.

Although he never married, Banneker did not have time to be lonely. He continued to work on the family farm, filling his spare time with reading, writing, and music. He even taught himself to play the flute and violin. In the evening, after the chores were done, he often played one of his instruments outdoors near his orchard.

Life became more exciting when the two Ellicott brothers and their families moved to Baltimore County to build mills along the Patapsco River. People for miles around watched with fascination as construction began. At first, Banneker watched from a distance. He had never seen such mechanical marvels. The milling operation was fully automated, driven by a clever use of machinery. Before long, however, his curiosity overcame his shyness, and he became acquainted with the Ellicotts. Soon he and his mother were providing much of the food and supplies needed by the workmen at the mill.

During the next several years, an unusually strong friendship developed between one of the young Ellicott boys and Benjamin Banneker. George Ellicott was fascinated by science and mathematics and soon discovered that Banneker was, too. Although Banneker was much older, George often visited him. The two became good friends while discussing what they were reading, their ideas, or their dreams.

One day George drove into Banneker's yard with a wagon filled with surprises. "Banneker!" he called. "Are you in there?"

Banneker appeared from around the back of the house where he had been tending to his apple orchard.

"I've got something for you, Banneker. I want you to keep these things for me for awhile." As he spoke, Ellicott began to unload his wagon, hauling several boxes of books into the house, and quickly returning for other things. Banneker stared in amazement as the young man grinned.

"What will I do with all this?" he asked, scratching his head.

"Oh, you'll figure it out soon enough!" By this time George had piled onto Banneker's dining table several globes, a set of drafting instruments, and a number of other tools. On his last trip to the wagon, George carefully lifted out the brass tubes of a telescope. Banneker stood speechless.

"I don't have time to show you how to use this stuff today," George shouted as he drove away. "But I'll be back in a month or so to explain it."

Banneker forgot about the rest of the day's work. He was too busy examining the things George had left. That night, when the stars came out, he set up the telescope and began to gaze at the heavens. "I have always loved to look up, but I never dreamed there was so much to see!" he cried to himself in wonder.

Night after night, he traded sleep for the stars. During the day, he studied astronomy books, trying to understand what he was seeing through the telescope. He also kept careful notes in his journals, comparing the positions of the stars from one evening to the next.

Long before Ellicott came back, Banneker had mastered the material in the books. He had even drawn a precise projection of an eclipse of the sun. This required many calculations involving logarithms, but Banneker did not give up. He worried that his farm needed attention, but he couldn't resist this chance to learn about astronomy.

One day Banneker had an idea. He would calculate an

ephemeris for an almanac. In colonial American life, an almanac was an almost indispensable source of information, the only way to know what time the sun would rise and set on a given day, for example. Farmers relied on it for advice on planting and the weather. Navigators needed it for tide schedules and for positions of fixed stars.

The ephemeris was the most crucial section of the almanac and the most difficult to compile. This collection of tables showing the day to day positions of the sun, moon, and planets had to be assembled with precise accuracy. The work demanded thousands of exact computations that had to be done over again each year.

More for his own pleasure than for any other reason, Banneker began to assemble an ephemeris. But when George Ellicott saw Banneker's work, he encouraged him to submit it for publication.

Banneker's almanacs were published from 1791 to 1797, and widely distributed throughout Pennsylvania, Maryland, Delaware, and Virginia. Recognized for their accuracy and value, they also proved that an African-American could be gifted in science and mathematics. The Societies for the Promotion of the Abolition of Slavery promoted the sale of the almanacs and used them in their arguments against slavery. Thomas Jefferson, then Secretary of State, sent Banneker a letter, complimenting him on his work.

When a site—now Washington, D.C.—was selected for the new United States capitol, Major Andrew Ellicott, George's father, was chosen to do the surveying of the boundaries. On his surveying team, he needed someone he could trust to accurately maintain the astronomical clock in the observatory tent. This was extremely important, because the heavens were the constant by which all other measurements would be guided. The work also would be cold and damp, requiring irregular hours throughout the night. Ellicott knew of only one man suited for the job—Benjamin Banneker.

Banneker was proud to have a part in the project, and he felt privileged to have such fine equipment at his disposal. But the work had been hard and tiring for a man of sixty, and this was the only time he was away from his little village in Maryland. Banneker, however, faithfully executed the assignment and his abilities as a surveyor and astronomer became widely known.

Banneker died after a long illness just a month before his seventy-fifth birthday. As his body was lowered into the grave on the family farm, his house mysteriously burst into flames. Everything he owned, including his manuscripts and the clock he built as a very young man, was destroyed. But his legacy of determination and dedication lives on even today.

CHARLES BABBAGE, 1792–1871, was a British mathematician, engineer, and inventor. His "engines" were the clear forerunners of today's calculators and computers.

The Computer's Grandfather

Charles Babbage hurried down the street to his workshop. He had a new idea about how one of the gears on his engine could be improved, and he wanted to try it out.

As Babbage rounded the corner of a brick building, he was stopped short by a small crowd of people. "All around the cobbler's bench, the monkey chased the weasel. . . ." Oh, no, thought Babbage. Not another organ grinder! As he tried to scoot past the cluster of people, he almost tripped on the furry little animal in costume that ran into his path, demanding a coin for its cup.

"Never!" he shouted at the monkey, swinging his arm as if to knock the little tin cup clear across the street. "Now get out of my way!"

The monkey scurried back to its owner, shifting its attention to several children offering it peanuts. Babbage, on the other hand, found himself out of breath and exasperated. For a moment, he couldn't remember where he was going or why.

"Those confounded organ grinders are defiling the whole city," he muttered. "Soon London will be one giant circus, and no one will be able to do any serious thinking."

When Babbage got to his workshop, he was surprised to find Ada Lovelace already there. She was so absorbed in studying his plans for the engine that she hardly looked up. "You know, Babbage, I think this is going to work!"

"Humph!" Babbage replied. "Had you been doubtful?"

"Not exactly," she explained. "I was so excited when you first showed me this design; I guess I have been afraid of finding something wrong with it. I've studied it carefully, and I'm glad to say it looks perfect to me."

"Just imagine, Ada, what this could mean to science and industry. Why, when I was in school, they gave us logarithm tables so full of errors a person was doomed to failure. Even then, I thought that if they had been calculated by machinery instead of by hand, they would have been more accurate. I mean, who wants to cross a bridge designed by an engineer who may have miscalculated his stress measurements?"

"I know," Ada agreed. "And won't it be wonderful when this engine generates accurate navigation tables?" She knew of several shipwrecks in the past five years that had been the result of inaccurate computations. The shipping industry depended heavily on such tables.

If anyone had suggested to Babbage that his partner in the difference engine project would be a woman, he would have howled with laughter. His was a complex design, difficult for even the smartest men he knew to comprehend. Ada and her mother had been introduced to him at a party. When he described his work, Ada listened in fascination.

"You see," he summarized, "I feed the first few entries into the machine. The machine notes the differences, and repeats the pattern indefinitely. When I crank the handle to turn the wheels, the differences are automatically added to obtain the next entry in the table."

Babbage was surprised at how quickly Ada understood and was pleased with her interest in actually seeing the plans. It was not long before she committed herself to help him realize his dream.

Babbage spread out his drawings and diagrams until the work table was covered. "I almost forgot. Late last night I had an idea about how this one set of gears could be changed. See what you think." Then he immersed himself in meticulously modifying a tiny section in each of the plans.

Several days later, Babbage was invited to a dinner for civic leaders and businessmen. Everyone was in a jovial mood, inspiring one of the men to tease Babbage.

"Hey Babbage, have you heard any good music on the street lately?" His companions laughed. Everyone knew about Babbage's campaign against street musicians, and against organ grinders in particular.

"As a matter of fact, I have, on the way over here this evening," Babbage grinned. "The musicians' tunes turned rather sour, however, when they saw me approaching." Babbage suddenly became solemn. "I'm thinking about taking them to court. They have absolutely no understanding of the damage they do."

"Damage?" asked his neighbor. "What kind of damage?"

"Well," said Babbage. "Suppose I'm considering a new invention, or developing plans for an intricate gear system. When I hear that terrible, tinny music from the street, I get so distracted I must lose at least twenty-five percent of my thoughts. It makes me so angry I start to feel violent. There's one fellow who plays under my window just to harass me. I warned him that next time I'll call the police and have him imprisoned!" Babbage slapped his open hand down on the table, rattling the silverware and china.

Several officials of the recently constructed railway, seated near Babbage, wisely tried to change the topic.

"So, Babbage, what do you think of our new mode of travel?"

"I'm for it, assuming they keep monkeys off the trains!"

His dinner companions began to discuss the new railway. The officials were concerned about the danger of trains hitting an animal or even a person. Some also were worried that pranksters might place objects in the paths of the trains. Babbage listened quietly. That night in his apartment, he drew up a plan. He would suggest that a strong frame called a cowcatcher be mounted on the front of the train, to push away any obstacle from the rails. Even if an animal or a careless person should be hit by the train at its top speed of twenty miles per hour, their lives would be spared. Surely someone hit would not complain about a mere broken leg!

Babbage's interest in train safety extended beyond his invention of the cowcatcher to a system of railroad crossing signals. His fascination with gears and wheels also led him to invent the first speedometer and an odometer to record how fast and how far a vehicle traveled.

Babbage was always looking for ways to make government and business more efficient. Once, he volunteered to do a study of the postal system. Mail throughout London was charged a variable rate, depending on how far it had to be carried. This was time-consuming for postal workers, and confusing for customers. After a week of analyzing the contents of mail bags in one district, Babbage concluded that it would be more efficient and economical if all letters were charged one flat rate. His findings resulted in a revolutionary overhaul of the postal system.

Babbage was officially listed as a professor at Cambridge. He never actually taught there, but he was allowed to do research and investigation using the title. This, and his reputation as an inventor, gave him a head start with government officials. When he proposed developing the difference engine, the British government provided funding and offered him a workshop. They knew that such a machine would make a tremendous contribution to society, and especially to military operations.

However, after spending eleven years and an enormous amount of money on the project, including his own inheritance, Babbage had built only one small section of the difference engine. He had encountered all sorts of difficulties. First, he had to have many of the parts and operating tools specially fabricated. Second, he kept changing the plans, inspired by ideas he thought would make a better product. This irritated and annoyed his co-workers, creating constant tension in the workshop. Finally, Babbage abandoned his plans for a difference engine because he had a better idea.

The idea took shape on a visit to France, where a weaver, J. M. Jacquard, had invented a revolutionary new process. Jacquard used punched cards on his loom to weave intricate designs into fabrics. Babbage was fascinated by the way the cards controlled the loom's movement. He wondered if the same idea would work on a new machine he had been considering.

Babbage set to work drawing up plans for his new dream, the analytical engine, a machine that would add, multiply, divide, and print. Information and instructions would be communicated to the machine through the codes on punched cards. The machine would call for new data from its storage bank.

Ada Lovelace supported Babbage's new plan. When he ran out of money, she donated some of her own. She wrote about the engine, explaining its mechanism so clearly that she was soon considered Babbage's chief assistant and spokesperson. In her clarification of the punched card process she said, "The analytical engine weaves algebraical patterns, just as the Jacquard loom weaves flowers and leaves."

Scientists and mathematicians from around the world came to study Babbage's plans. Most of them believed that the idea was sound, but they shook their heads at the thought of actually building such a machine. "It would take too much time," they said. "There are no craftsmen to build the parts," they worried. "Who will pay for it?" they wondered.

Charles Babbage spent his entire fortune and most of his life in an attempt to build the analytical engine. After his death, his son worked nearly thirty years on the project, but the dream was never realized. The engine was simply too advanced for the times. There was not enough money, not enough expertise, and not enough time to build such a massive machine.

Like many other pioneers, Babbage never saw the result of his dreams. But his work was not a waste of time nor money. The fundamental ideas he established became the basis for building the world's first working computers. Later computer designers relied heavily on his plans.

When Babbage was a young man studying at Cambridge University, he and his two best friends, John Hershel and George Peacock, made a pact. They solemnly agreed to "do their best to leave the world wiser than they found it." Together they founded the Analytical Society, which had a profoundly positive effect on the future development of mathematics in England. Hershel went on to become an outstanding astronomer. In addition to his mathematical work, Peacock entered the ministry. And Babbage? While his interests ranged from promoting life insurance to identifying lighthouses by their beacons, Babbage's consuming passion was mathematical machines. For that reason, he is sometimes called the "grandfather of the modern computer."

MARY FAIRFAX SOMERVILLE, 1780–1872, was a Scottish mathematician and scientist whose books became popular texts. She was admired for the way she compiled and explained the scientific knowledge of her day.

The Mystery of *X* and *Y*

"Capital M-a-g-n-a Capital C-a-r-t-a. Pronounced 'Magna Carta.' The great charter of English liberties, delivered June 19, 1215, by King John on the demand of the English barons," recited Anne. "Also, any document that secures liberty and rights."

"Anne," Mary whispered, cupping her hand over her mouth. "Do you think Miss Primrose has ever heard of the Magna Carta?"

"I'm sure she has. Why do you ask?" Anne whispered back. Then she saw Mary's mischievous grin. "You'd never know it, the way we have to work, right?"

"She's kind enough, I guess. But you'd think there would be a law against expecting eleven- and twelve-year-old girls to memorize pages from Samuel Johnson's dictionary!"

"I know. It's awfully tedious. I always hope it's at least interesting. Last week I got a page of R's that kept me confused for days," Anne groaned.

"These braces we have to wear don't fit my definition of liberty, either," Mary hissed to her friend across the aisle. "Sometimes I can hardly breathe."

Mary Fairfax and her friend Anne were students at Miss Primrose's boarding school for girls. Each morning before breakfast the girls were helped into elaborate steel frames to guarantee they would sit straight. Each contraption included supports to keep the chest upright, metal pieces to keep the shoulder blades firmly pulled back, and another section to hold the chin up. The girls hated the restriction and pain caused by this custom—even the prettiest dresses worn over this scaffold looked lumpy and misshapen.

Mary was especially miserable at Miss Primrose's. She had always been free to roam as she pleased at home. But her father thought she was growing up too wild, "like a savage," he'd said. He sent Mary to school to "become civilized." The other girls attending the school told her that she would get used to it, but Mary thought this kind of "civilization" was not for her.

"Girls! Let's keep our minds on our lessons," ordered Miss Primrose. "Mary, Anne, no more talking, unless of course you want to memorize two more pages before dinner!"

Mary sighed and continued to read. "Magnetite, m-a-g-n-e-t-i-t-e. Isometric black iron oxide, found in octahedral and dodecahedral crystals, sometimes found in beach sand." She tried to go on to the next entry, but she could not concentrate. She was thinking about the beautiful beaches on the seacoast near her home in Burntisland, Scotland. When the tide was out, she would spend hours combing the sand for jellyfish, crabs, and sea urchins. While other girls played with dolls, Mary much preferred to be outdoors exploring. Sometimes she collected beautiful rocks and minerals, and now she wondered if she had some magnetite in her box of treasures at home.

Even though she was still at her desk, Mary almost could hear her mother calling her at home in the evening. "Mary! Mary Fairfax, where are you? It's getting dark. Time to come in now."

"Coming, Mother. Just a few more minutes."

Then she would scan the horizon, gazing toward the setting sun. She liked to pretend that she could see her father's ship approaching. He was an admiral in the Scottish navy, and would use a different port, but it was fun to imagine.

On a very dark night at home, Mary liked to sit in her favorite attic window. Opening to the north, the window gave Mary a wonderful view of the stars. If she were feeling sad or melancholy, it was a comforting, tranquil spot in which to think. If she were feeling energetic, on the other hand, the attic window opened up a world of scientific possibility. Often she thought about the navigators at sea, and wondered if they watched the same stars as she.

A tap on the shoulder brought Mary back to Miss Primrose's room.

"Magpie, m-a-g-p-i-e. A long-tailed black and white bird related to jays and crows. Usually builds its nest on the ground."

What happened to the eggs in that nest, Mary wondered. She was especially fond of birds, and loved to watch from a distance as their eggs got ready to hatch. She felt that some birds in the family garden were almost like friends. Maybe she didn't yet read and write very well, but she knew all about the different species of birds.

After one year at Miss Primrose's school, Mary's parents agreed to let her come home. With a great sigh of relief, she left the steel restraints behind, too, returning to the Scottish seacoast with a new appreciation of freedom and nature. Although their attempts at "civilizing" Mary were not a complete success, her parents were pleased that she could now read and write reasonably well.

Mary had also gained a new appreciation for learning, though she never came to respect Miss Primrose's methods of teaching. Mary's mother now allowed her to choose books from the family library to read. She also began to study Latin and Greek, and taught herself the basics of these languages. One of the books in her father's library especially intrigued her. It was about navigation and charting the constellations. From that book, Mary discovered that if she wanted to really learn about the stars that she viewed from her attic window, she would have to learn more about mathematics.

One winter, Mary and her mother spent several months in Edinburgh, where Mary went to writing school and studied some simple arithmetic. She also took piano lessons, and became a disciplined student. Playing the piano was to give her joy for many years.

"Mary," asked her friend Julia one day, "have you seen this issue of *The Ladies' Diary* yet?" She sat beside Mary on the porch step.

"No, I haven't. May I look with you?"

The girls pored over the fashion magazine like typical teenagers. Julia was quick to point out the latest in stylish dresses and shoes, but Mary had her eye on something else.

It was customary for magazines like *The Ladies' Diary* to intersperse illustrations with riddles and puzzles for the entertainment of readers. Often the puzzles required solving simple arithmetic problems.

"Look, Julia. What's this?" asked Mary, pointing to a problem on the page. "It looks like arithmetic, but it has *x*'s and *y*'s in it. Do you know what they mean?"

"Really? Let me see." Julia held the magazine up toward the light and squinted. "Now I remember. Miss Olgivie said that it's a kind of arithmetic called *algebra*. But she didn't know any more about it."

All those *x*'s and *y*'s pricked Mary's curiosity. She determined to find out about this algebra, but there was no one to ask. After awhile, she began to think her quest was hopeless, until the day she sat in on her younger brother's tutoring session. Mary was in the parlor sewing when Mr. Gaw arrived to teach Henry mathematics.

Since sewing was a quiet occupation, Mary was allowed to stay during the tutoring session. She went on with her own business, listening almost absentmindedly. When Henry was slow to answer Mr. Gaw's question, Mary blurted out the answer without thinking.

Mr. Gaw was shocked. "How did you know that?" he asked. "This is a very difficult concept, not one a girl would understand!"

Though Mr. Gaw was surprised, he was not upset, and quickly perceived that Mary was more eager to learn than Henry. After this, he always saved a little time in the lesson to answer her questions, and to explain what she had not been able to figure out on her own.

For some time, Mary had desperately wanted a copy of Euclid's *Elements*. She had heard that Euclid was the key to mathematical thinking and research. Because girls were not welcomed in many bookstores, she persuaded Mr. Gaw to buy a copy for her. He also brought his eager student a book about algebra. Now she would understand those x's and y's!

Mary established a daily schedule to make sure she used her time wisely. Every morning she rose early. For the first five hours of the morning, she practiced piano. Then she did her housework and chores, and sometimes painted in the garden. In the evenings, she loved to go dancing or attend concerts with friends. At night, when the house was quiet, she got out her mathematics books and studied as long as she could.

Mary's routine was disrupted when the housekeeper complained about the family's candle supply. Candles were mysteriously disappearing faster than she could replenish them. With a little investigation, Mary's parents discovered the culprit.

"Mary, you know studying this late is not good for you," her father began. "We have warned you before, have we not?"

"Yes, Father. I'm sorry," she said softly.

"Your mother and I are responsible for your health. From now on, we will come up to your room at bedtime to collect your candles. You are expected to go to bed then." He looked into her eyes. "Do you understand?"

"Yes, Father, I understand."

Mary obediently went to bed on time. But by then she had almost mastered many of Euclid's ideas. So when she crawled into bed and closed her eyes, she practiced solving problems in her mind. Her father had said she must go to bed, but he hadn't said she had to go to sleep!

In 1804, Mary was married, but her husband died a short time later. Her second husband, Dr. William Somerville, a surgeon in the British navy, was a wonderful companion and support. Unlike most men of his day, he was happy to see women becoming educated and developing their intelligence. He was proud of Mary and loved nothing more than helping her.

Mary Somerville was forty-seven years old when she began her most important project. She was approached by the High Chancellor of Britain with a unique proposal. The French mathematician, Laplace, had written a valuable book called *Celestial Mechanics*. Somerville was asked to translate this book into English and to rewrite it in such a way that it could be understood even by persons who were not scientists.

Mary Somerville was reluctant to tackle this assignment. "I don't know if I am capable of the technical aspects," she said modestly.

"Mrs. Somerville," the chancellor assured her, "we have the utmost confidence in you. Please give it a try."

"If I do, you must make me a solemn promise."

"Yes. What is it?" he asked.

"My work must be done in complete secrecy. No one but you and my husband shall know I am working on it. Then, if I fail, the manuscript shall be burned."

When she began to work, Somerville found it difficult to concentrate. She was a mother and wanted to spend time with her children. She had household duties to perform, and visitors to entertain. "A man," she said, "could use his work as an excuse to be left alone, but a woman has to contend with interruptions."

It took Somerville four years to complete *The Mechanism of the Heavens*, which was a remarkable success. Her interpretations of Laplace's ideas made them accessible to a larger audience. Readable and practical, the popular book was used for many years as a text in higher mathematics and astronomy courses. Even Laplace was pleased. He often said Mary Somerville was the only woman in the world who understood his work.

Research and writing became a constant in Somerville's life. She wrote and published a book on the physical sciences, and another on physical geography. When she was almost ninety, she published a book on molecular and microscopic science. Each of her books reinforced one of her strongest opinions: all of mathematics and science is inter-connected.

Mary Somerville received many honors and awards during her lifetime. She was invited to join several prestigious scientific associations, sometimes as their first woman member. For many years, she received an annual pension from the king of England to support her work. Statues were erected to honor her, and mathematicians and scientists throughout Europe acknowledged their indebtedness to her.

In her own quiet way, Mary Somerville worked to provide more opportunities for women. She believed that women should receive the same education as men, and she was the first person to sign John Stuart Mill's petition to give women the right to vote. Still, she must have felt frustrated at times.

Mary Somerville and her husband eventually moved to Italy, hoping the warmer climate would improve his health. After his death, she stayed on for the remainder of her life, comfortable within her circle of friends and associates. Naples was a popular city for scientists because it contained one of the finest, most powerful telescopes in Europe. In 1834, mathematicians and scientists gathered in expectation to view a remarkable comet. Many people were eager to hear Mary Somerville's account of the sighting because her insights were always refreshing and enlightening. But Mary Somerville did not get to see the comet. The telescope had been built in a Jesuit monastery, and women, even if they were mathematicians or scientists, were not allowed on the property.

NIELS HENRIK ABEL (AH-bul), 1802–1829, was Norway's most famous mathematician. He proved that it was impossible to find an algebraic formula to solve general fifth degree equations. His work in group theory had important implications for modern number theory.

The Overlooked Genius

A fresh sea breeze cooled the air as the children scrambled to kick the ball. "Hey, Hans," Niels shouted. "Kick it to Peder for a change."

Little Peder grinned in delight. He drew his leg back for a big kick. Before the ball got to him, however, he lost his balance and fell into the grass.

"Good job, Peder," his older brothers laughed. "You'll get it next time for sure!"

Just then their father came striding up the path. He had been visiting his parishioners in their small Norwegian village. Pastor Abel was always welcomed by his neighbors; he was well informed about politics and literature, which made his visits interesting as well as encouraging. Although he taught his children at home in addition to his other work, he was never too tired to play with them.

"Niels," he called with a wave of his arm, "I need to speak with you."

Niels hurried to his father's side. While the other children scrambled into the house to get ready for the evening meal, they went for a walk.

"This afternoon I made arrangements for you to go to school in Oslo," Niels' father began. "What do you think of that?"

"I . . . uh . . . I don't know, Father. I guess I haven't thought about it yet."

"You know, son, they have some fine teachers at the Cathedral School. Now that you are twelve years old, I think you need to learn more than I can teach you." He stopped and turned to face Niels. "Are you willing to go?"

"Yes, Father. I'm willing. But it may be difficult to get used to a teacher other than you," he grinned. Then he considered the other adjustments he would have to make. "This means that I will also be boarding at Cathedral, right? Are you sure we can afford it? I mean, with all the other children at home and . . . and the famine."

His father patted Niels' back. "Don't you worry about that, son. Everything has been taken care of. If you're willing, you'll start next month."

Niels liked school. He enjoyed learning Latin, history, and geography, and though not an outstanding student, he passed all of his classes. The other boys liked Niels, often inviting him to play chess or cards. Occasionally, they all attended the theater to see a play. This was Niels' favorite pastime; he loved the excitement and spectacle of the theater.

Only one aspect of school was unpleasant for Niels. The teachers had been taught that the only way to maintain order in the classroom was through physical force. There were few limits or policies on discipline in those days, but teachers usually resorted to beating a student only when other methods of punishment were ineffective. When Mr. Bader was hired, however, the boys soon knew they were in for trouble. A short-tempered man, he had little tolerance for disobedience or laziness. If he called on someone who could not answer his question, he would march down the aisle and hit that boy with a stick. Some of the boys were young and had trouble learning certain subjects, but Mr. Bader accepted no excuses. If they stumbled or gave an incorrect answer, he would laugh and ridicule them. If they cried, he attacked them more savagely.

Niels and his friends often discussed the teacher's tactics.

"Did you see how Mr. Bader clubbed George today?" Carl asked. "He'll be sore for weeks!"

Niels shook his head sadly. "It made me angry, Carl. I saw the wild look in his eyes. He is a troubled man. My father used to say that a troubled man should never be a teacher. One of these days I'm afraid he'll lose control."

Niels was right. In 1818, Mr. Bader beat and kicked a student so severely that eight days later the boy died. At first, the teacher was only scolded. But when the other boys threatened to leave school if he was not fired, the school board finally took action.

This was a horrible incident, but something good came out of it for Niels Abel—a new teacher. Bernt Holmboe was an enthusiastic young man who loved music, literature, and mathematics. He believed that if a teacher made learning enjoyable, the students would be well-behaved. With that attitude, he quickly succeeded in winning the students' respect and admiration.

One day Mr. Holmboe arranged to meet Niels Abel after class. "Niels," he began, "I would like to congratulate you on your fine marks in mathematics."

"Thank you, sir."

"By the way," the teacher continued. "I have several books here I'd like to loan you. I think you'll find them interesting. Let me know what you think."

That night in his room, Niels examined Mr. Holmboe's books, a calculus text by Leonard Euler, and two volumes by the mathematicians Lagrange and Laplace. Hours later, Niels' history assignment was still unread. The books in mathematics had captured his imagination most powerfully, challenging him to think in a new way. Niels decided he only wanted to study mathematics.

When Niels was eighteen years old, his father died. The family had always been poor, but now the responsibility to provide for them fell on Niels. If he could just graduate from the university, he reasoned, he could get a job as a professor and make enough money to support his mother and the five younger children.

At first, officials at the University of Oslo weren't sure if they should accept Abel as a student. His scores on the entrance exam were not very good, except in mathematics. However, since his mathematics scores were the highest of anyone taking the test, they decided to give him a chance.

Some of Abel's professors knew that he had to support his mother, so they set up and contributed to a scholarship fund. Abel responded by practically absorbing the library's entire collection of advanced mathematical works during his first year there.

When Abel was only nineteen years old and still a student, he solved a problem that had perplexed mathematicians for three centuries. Earlier mathematicians had discovered formulas to solve third and fourth degree equations, but no formula had been found to solve the general fifth degree equation. Abel was intrigued by this challenge. First he labored long hours researching work done by others. For a while, he thought he had found a formula, but further analysis proved him wrong.

Rather than let discouragement dampen his spirit, Abel made his mistakes work for him. He proved that it was impossible to find an algebraic formula to solve general fifth degree equations. This was a remarkable discovery, one that would change the very basis of mathematical thinking.

But most mathematicians had never heard of Abel. They didn't believe someone from a little village in Norway would have a genuine proof. What's more, no one would publish his discovery. Finally, he borrowed money to pay to have it printed as a small pamphlet. Because of cost, he had to condense his reasoning into six short pages. In the process, the arguments became hard to follow. Naturally, Abel became discouraged when great mathematicians like Gauss casually tossed his work aside.

At the university, Abel devoted himself fully to his studies. Occasionally, however, he took time off to go to the theater or to travel. On a rare vacation in Copenhagen, he saw an interesting-looking young woman at a dance. He found her red hair and freckles quite charming and asked a friend to introduce him.

"Miss Kemp," said Abel's friend. "I'd like you to meet Niels Abel. He's visiting from Oslo."

"How do you do?" she said. "My name is Christine."

Abel was shy, but Christine made him feel comfortable.

"Would you like to dance?" he asked.

"Thank you," she said, taking his arm.

On the dance floor, Abel hesitated, then slipped his arm around Christine's waist as she placed her feet near his. The music began. He looked at her and she looked at him. After a few moments of awkwardness, they both burst out laughing. Neither one of them knew how to dance!

Christine was a lovely girl, bright and energetic. She and Abel decided to become better acquainted through letters.

The next year, Abel located a family near him who needed a governess. Christine was perfect for the position, and this gave the young couple an opportunity to spend time together. Soon they became engaged, but decided not to marry until Abel had a position that could support the two of them as well as his mother and siblings. Unfortunately, such a job was not easily found.

In 1825, the Norwegian government granted Abel funds for a year of travel and study in France and Germany. In Berlin, Abel met August Crelle, an amateur mathematician who dreamt of publishing a journal in which mathematicians could share their discoveries and ideas. He was impressed with Abel's work, and wanted Abel to assist him with the journal. He promised to try to help Abel get a job at the University of Berlin, or even to appoint him editor of the journal if he could find financial backing.

The position in Berlin did not materialize. After Abel's year of travel, he returned to Norway, still without a job. Abel didn't let poverty keep him from working. Even though he always was scraping together funds to send to his mother, he managed to focus on his research. He wrote a series of articles for Crelle's *Journal*. In the first of these, he expanded on his earlier proof of the impossibility of solving any fifth degree equation with an algebraic formula. Eventually, mathematicians throughout Europe began to notice Abel and seriously consider his work.

Abel, meanwhile, was barely getting by in Norway by tutoring and filling in as a substitute teacher in astronomy classes. He wondered if he and Christine would be able to marry. It seemed as if poverty were a giant pit with no way out. Then, in January, he began to feel sick.

At first, Abel thought he had a cold. But soon he became weak and lost weight. Finally, a doctor told him he had pneumonia. Bed rest was essential.

The family Christine worked for insisted that Abel should stay with them while he was recuperating. Christine could help care for him, and everyone would worry less. That is just what happened. On days when he felt strong enough, Abel sat up in bed and worked on his projects.

"Christine," he said one day in March, "I've been thinking about that play we saw together in Copenhagen. You know, the one where the curtain would not lift?"

"Yes, Niels, I remember. Why are you thinking of that?" she asked.

"Well, in some ways my life is like that," he explained. "I have worked hard. I have submitted manuscripts to all the right people. I have tried to publish my findings. But it does no good if people do not see it. I feel like the powerful drama is still behind the curtain."

Christine smiled and touched his hand. Tears filled her eyes as she thought of their unfulfilled dreams.

Abel continued. "I wish I knew of a way to thank you for your kindness to me. I could not have asked for a more wonderful fiancée. I'm so sorry things turned out this way."

"Sh-h-h, Niels," she hushed. "Don't talk nonsense. You could have had any woman in Europe as a fiancée, and you know it. Now lie back down and get some rest."

But Abel did not get better. He had tuberculosis, and there was no cure.

Abel wrote a secret letter to his good friend, Baltazar Keilhau. "I have a special request of you. Take care of Christine for me, will you? She has been such a loving nurse. She deserves some happiness, and I think you two would be good for each other. I would be pleased if you would marry her."

On April 6, 1829, Niels Abel died. He was twenty-six years old. Two days later, a letter arrived from Berlin. August Crelle had just received the good news that the University of Berlin would hire Abel. Crelle was certain the position would solve Abel's financial problems and firmly establish his influence among European mathematicians.

This letter was not the only good news that came too late. A paper that Abel had submitted years earlier to the French Academy was finally "found" and evaluated. When the leaders of the prestigious society studied it, they recognized its brilliance by awarding Abel the Grand Prize in Mathematics. The work he had been so proud of was finally published.

Abel's friend, Keilhau, had never met Christine. After Abel died, Keilhau wrote her a letter and proposed. "It would be a good way to honor our dear Niels," he suggested. Christine accepted, and they were married.

The French mathematician, Hermite, was grieved to learn of Abel's death. After reviewing all of the articles Abel had written and the discoveries he had made, Hermite said, "Abel has left mathematicians something to keep them busy for five hundred years."

ADA BYRON LOVELACE, 1815–1852, was a British mathematician, best known as the inventor of computer programming. The computer language ADA is named in tribute to her work.

Conducting the Computer Symphony

"Oh, listen, girls. Isn't the music divine?"

"It's the most wonderful I've ever heard, Elinor. But the whole evening is marvelous," gushed Louisa. "Look at all the beautiful gowns. Have you ever seen so many jewels sparkling in one room?"

Elinor and Louisa stood on their tiptoes and craned their necks to scan the ballroom. Their friend Ada, however, seemed to be lost in her own thoughts.

"There are plenty of handsome young men to dance with, too." Louisa giggled. "Which one do you want, Ada?"

Ada did not seem to hear.

"Ada? Ada, we're talking to you!"

Ada jumped as though startled. "What? I'm sorry. I was thinking about something else. What did you say?"

"Oh, so that's it," Louisa teased. "You've already picked out a beau!"

"Who is it, Ada?" Elinor begged. "Tell us who you're looking for. Maybe we can help you spot him!"

Ada didn't even smile at their joke. She was trying to see past the billowing taffeta skirts and fancy hairdos to find the one person she had hoped to meet at the party.

"I'll see you girls later, okay?" she said, slipping away into the crowd before they had a chance to ask more questions or protest.

She had not made much progress in crossing the ballroom when Ada heard her mother's voice behind her. "Ada! I'm so glad I found you. Come quickly. There's someone I want you to meet."

Ada followed her mother to an elaborately decorated alcove where, arm in arm, they were received by the queen of England. After Ada and her mother curtsied and extended their hands, Mrs. Byron proudly introduced her daughter to Queen Adelaide. "I call her The Young Lioness, your Majesty," she said with a smile. "She's beautiful but feisty!"

Queen Adelaide responded warmly. "Aren't you the very image of your father!" she marveled. "You certainly have his dark good looks. Did you also inherit his poetic inclinations?"

Ada smiled and practiced the etiquette her mother had taught her, but she was relieved when the audience with the queen was over. Ada's father, Lord Byron, had been a well-known poet. Even though she could not remember him, she benefited in social settings by having his name. She was comfortable around rich and famous people, but, if she had to choose, she preferred people who were interesting, people who enjoyed thinking. As they left the Queen's alcove, she reminded her mother that there was only one introduction that would make the evening a success in her mind. She wanted to meet Mary Somerville.

"Oh, that's right, you do," answered her mother, "though I don't understand why meeting her should be so important to a seventeen-year-old girl after meeting the queen. Well, all right, then, I did just see her." She led Ada past the refreshment table to a quiet corner of the room.

Ada's heart pounded with excitement as she took the hand of Mary Somerville. "How do you do?" she blurted. "I've been wanting to meet you for *years*!"

Mrs. Somerville laughed. "It can't have been *that* long, dear. You're not that old!"

Ada quickly explained that she had read Mrs. Somerville's book, *The Mechanism of the Heavens*. "I'm a student of mathematics myself," she added proudly. "Of course, I'm just beginning, but I'd be ever so happy if you would take me on as your pupil!"

Mary Somerville did just that. When Ada had questions about something she'd read or a problem she'd been working on, she often went to Mrs. Somerville's home to seek her advice. Mrs. Somerville encouraged her to keep up her work in mathematics, and suggested books for Ada to read.

"Have you ever found yourself torn between two loves?" Ada asked Mrs. Somerville one day.

"I'm not sure I know what you mean, Ada."

"Well, I love mathematics, and I think I'm good at it. But I also love music. You know, I've studied the piano and the violin for years. My teachers think I can be a professional musician if I devote myself to it. How do I decide?"

Mrs. Somerville thought for awhile before she spoke. "Ada, only you can choose. Perhaps your family would find music a more acceptable career. Still, your mother is something of a mathematician herself, and she will surely understand if you follow that dream. I can't tell you what to do. It's hard, but you must search deep down inside yourself for the answer."

"I was afraid you'd say that," said Ada, smiling. "But thank you." Then, as an afterthought, she added brightly, "Maybe someday I'll find a way to combine mathematics and music. What do you think about that idea?"

"We'll see," answered Mrs. Somerville with a twinkle in her eye.

At another party several months later, Mrs. Somerville introduced Ada to Charles Babbage. "Mr. Babbage is working on a machine," explained Mrs. Somerville. "Something he calls a *difference engine*. I think you'd find it fascinating, especially because you enjoy anything mechanical."

Soon after that, Ada and her mother were invited to Babbage's workshop, where he described his project. He was building a machine that would be capable of calculating tables of numbers by computing their differences. At that time, all of the logarithmic, navigation, and financial tables were calculated by hand, which was extremely time consuming, and filled with errors. When Ada saw the machine, she immediately recognized its tremendous potential. She began to work with Babbage and to support his efforts.

Mrs. Somerville also introduced Ada to another person, Lord William King, a college friend of her son. Mrs. Somerville thought that he and Ada would be a good match. After getting to know each other, Ada and the young man agreed. Shortly after they married, William was named the Earl of Lovelace, making Ada the Countess of Lovelace.

Women in the early 1800s rarely studied mathematics or

science, so Ada Lovelace was fortunate to have a friend and model like Mary Somerville. She also was blessed with a husband who supported her in pursuing her interests. Later, when he was elected to the Royal Society, he copied by hand information from scientific books and papers in the Society's library, which Ada needed for her research. Women were not allowed in the library.

Although she had many other interests, Ada Lovelace continued to assist Charles Babbage. After many years of working on the difference engine, he abandoned it for a better plan—the analytical engine. This machine would be able to do much more than generate tables. It would perform a variety of functions by receiving commands from a series of punched cards. Babbage got his idea from a weaving loom designed by J. M. Jacquard. If the cards could tell the loom which threads to pick up, Babbage reasoned they could direct the machine as to which gears to operate.

Ada Lovelace had a remarkable ability to imagine what was going on in Babbage's mind. Her suggestions often helped him, and she even gave him financial support when his funding ran out. The plans for his engine drew attention from around the world, although it had not yet been built.

The first public explanation of how Babbage's machine would work was published by an Italian mathematician in 1842. Ada Lovelace proposed translating the article into English. Because she knew so much about the capabilities of the engine, her translation would include some additional notes. As the writing project progressed, those notes became more and more extensive. By the time she finished, the paper was three times as long as the original article, and much more useful. Babbage insisted on publishing it, but Lovelace refused to sign her name. Women of her social class were not expected to publish, especially not on such a complicated topic. Finally, she did agree to sign, but only her initials. It took over thirty years for the public to discover who the author was.

In this important paper, Lovelace described how Babbage's machine would work. She also outlined a range of programming techniques through which many mathematical operations could be achieved. She illustrated methods she had developed to solve complex problems, and she reminded the world of the machine's major limitation. It would not be able to think!

When she was about thirty-five, Lovelace became ill.

"Annabelle, would you bring me some of my headache powder?" Ada asked one day, as she stretched out on the sofa.

"Is it a bad one, Mother?" her daughter asked softly.

"I'm afraid so. Sometimes I wonder if the superstitions I've heard all my life are true."

In the nineteenth century, it was generally believed that women were too frail for intellectual endeavors. A woman who ventured to study or think too deeply was in danger of losing her health. Parents often shielded their little girls from education and restricted their reading in an effort to protect them.

"Annabelle, I don't really believe it," Ada said firmly. "I would probably be sicker if I did nothing but stitching and cooking. Lots of men get sick, too. And think of Mary Somerville! She's past seventy and healthy as can be. No one has had more mental exertion than she!"

In truth, Lovelace had rarely been healthy, even as a child. She often suffered migraine headaches, and occasionally a mysterious illness left her paralyzed for weeks at a time. But she never used illness as an excuse to quit trying. Instead, she filled her good days with a whirlwind of activities.

"Annabelle, have I ever told you how I loved to dance?"

"Yes, Mother, but tell me again."

"I don't mean to brag, but everyone said I was the best. When we had parties—I was only a child, maybe eleven or twelve years old—I danced like a grown-up. The other girls were so jealous." She paused to massage her temples, "Honey, would you mind getting me a cool damp cloth?"

Annabelle gently spread the soothing cloth on her mother's forehead. "How did you get to be such a good dancer?" she asked, hoping that talking would distract her mother from the pain.

"I think it was my gymnastics training," explained Ada. "Most of the girls were not interested in physical activity, but I loved it. I trained every day I could. That developed my muscles and coordination, and helped me become a strong and poised dancer. The horseback riding helped, too. Riding develops a sense of rhythm, don't you think?"

Annabelle treasured the times spent with her mother. She knew that Ada's health was failing, that it wasn't just a headache. The doctors had diagnosed cancer, and confined Ada to bed. Sometimes, when the pain subsided, Ada would sit up on the side of the bed and call for Annabelle. Then the two would play duets on the piano, which had been placed next to her bed.

"Annabelle, I've been thinking."

"About what, Mother?"

"About Babbage's engine. You know, I think those punched cards could be programmed to write and play music. I've always wanted to find a way to combine my love for music with my love for mathematics. I think I may have it figured out," she grinned. "Now, wouldn't that be something!"

SONYA KOVALEVSKY (kah-vuh-LEV-ski), 1850–1891, was a Russian mathematician who worked with infinite series. She also made a significant contribution to the understanding of Saturn's rings, and enhanced the methods of mathematical research.

The Lessons on the Wall

"Pssst, Sonya. Are you in there?"

A light tapping followed the whisper.

"Sonya, let me in. It's me, Aniuta. Can't you hear me?"

Sonya came back to reality with a start. Rushing to the door, she opened it just wide enough for her sister to enter.

"I'm sorry, Aniuta. I didn't hear you at first. I think I've found where the page continues, near the corner."

"Oh, you're reading the wallpaper again, are you? I don't understand what's so fascinating about some old calculus notes. Why don't you try reading a book for a change?"

"Well, it's not my fault that Mother and Father papered my walls with that stuff, is it? Besides, I find my wallpaper far more interesting than your roses and lilies," she teased, knowing how much Aniuta hated those gaudy flowers.

"Don't get me started on that!" Aniuta laughed.

The sound of familiar footsteps in the hallway abruptly ended their laughter, and they all but held their breath until the governess passed. Their strict English governess forbade the girls from seeing each other during the day, believing it would disrupt their lessons too much. Even though Aniuta was six years older than Sonya, the sisters were good friends. They had to sneak around their house behind their governess' back, but they both thought it was worth it.

When their father, General Krukovsky, retired from military service, he had moved the family to this large estate near St. Petersburg. He thought it would be good for the family to be spread throughout the old castle, and chose rooms for himself in the tower. Aniuta and their mother settled upstairs, while their younger brother, Fedya, lived in a separate wing with his tutor. Sonya was stuck with the governess on the main floor.

The ancient castle they called home was located in a remote, isolated area near the Lithuanian border. Sometimes at night the children were awakened by the sinister howling of wolves. Perhaps to soften the harsh, cold landscape, the parents ordered fancy wallpaper for all the rooms. Someone made a mistake in measuring, however, and the paper was gone by the time the decorators got to Sonya's room.

General Krukovsky did not like to admit mistakes, and refused to order more paper. He had just the thing for Sonya's room, he said. On an ambitious impulse years earlier, he had ordered a huge set of lithographed lectures on differential and integral calculus, intending to study the subject on his own. After all, his wife's father was an eminent German mathematician, and it would never hurt to make a good impression. But the sheets of notes remained untouched. They would, however, make a perfect wall-covering, the general decided.

Most young girls might have objected, but Sonya quickly became interested in the strange scribbles on her wall. She spent hours trying to decipher the formulas, and challenged herself to mentally put the pages in order. When her governess punished her by sending her to her room, she forgot about her loneliness, and instead became absorbed in the patterns and problems around her.

One day Aniuta told Sonya some good news. "Guess what, Sonya!"

"What?" she asked.

"Uncle Peter is coming to visit tonight. I heard Father telling Fedya."

Sonya was thrilled. Of all her relatives, Uncle Peter was definitely the favorite. He seemed to have a special affection for Sonya, too. When she was three or four years old, he used to toss her up into the air and catch her until she was weak with laughter. Then he would gently set her on his lap and tell her all sorts of fascinating stories.

Now that she was older, Uncle Peter was the one adult who truly listened to her; she felt that she could trust his advice.

"How are your lessons going, Sonya?" Uncle Peter inquired after dinner.

"They're fine, Uncle Peter. Language study is going well, and my tutor is convinced that I have a future as a writer. Last week I wrote a one-act play that he thinks has potential."

"Good for you. I've always suspected you would be famous someday."

"But I don't know if that's what I really want. I do enjoy writing, but I think I would rather study mathematics. It seems to come more naturally for me. I can concentrate on problems for hours and not even realize that time is passing." Sonya paused a moment, and turned her hazel brown eyes up to her uncle. "Do you think I should continue writing? Does a woman have a chance in mathematics?"

Uncle Peter's advice became Sonya's lifetime encouragement. "You must follow your heart, Sonya. Pursue what truly interests you, regardless of the obstacles. If you choose mathematics, you should know that it won't be easy," he added softly. "You will probably have to leave Russia to study. But the joy will be worth the struggle."

With this hope, Sonya began to work. She requested books on physics and trigonometry, and taught herself these subjects. Her father bought her a microscope, and she spent hours studying biology in her room.

When Sonya was eighteen, the family moved to St. Petersburg so that she and Fedya could attend school. They had outgrown their tutors and needed more advanced training. Sonya enrolled in calculus. On the first day, she was surprised at how familiar everything seemed. The professor explained the concepts slowly and carefully. Although Sonya had never studied calculus, it was as if she had seen it all before. Suddenly she remembered the formulas on her old wallpaper, and everything made sense!

Sonya was soon ready for university study, but the universities in Russia at that time did not admit women. Many young women found that their only alternative was to move to one of the European countries where there were more opportunities for women. But social custom would not allow a woman to travel or live abroad unaccompanied. Aniuta was not really interested in studying, but she volunteered to help Sonya concoct a plan.

"Remember our friend Maria? Let's do what she did—find a man to marry, and travel with him!"

"Are you serious, Aniuta?"

"Why not? If I married a man and went abroad, you could come along as my sister and live with us. It's a perfect plan!"

"But who would you marry? You don't even have a boyfriend. I hope you haven't forgotten that," she said with a small smile.

"Maria said she could find someone for me—just a business arrangement," Aniuta explained. "We wouldn't live together, of course."

Sonya and Aniuta continued to scheme, trying to think of men Aniuta could marry. After several months of investigation, they were introduced to Vladimir Kovalevsky, a paleontology student, and eventually told him about their idea. He thought carefully about their proposition, and finally agreed, on one condition: he wanted to marry Sonya, not Aniuta. This was highly unusual, since Aniuta was the older sister, but the girls were pleased to find a ticket to freedom.

Their father, the General, was not so pleased. In fact, he refused to allow Sonya to marry. She knew that arguing with him was pointless, so she devised still another plan. After leaving her father a note, she packed a few things and left home.

"Dear Father," the note said, "I am sorry to disappoint you this way. You leave me no other choice if I am to get my education. Vladimir and I are planning to elope."

This was just a bluff, but it worked for Sonya. Her father would not tolerate an elopement; it would be an embarrassment for the entire family. He immediately departed for Vladimir's apartment, where he granted his permission for the marriage. Vladimir and Sonya were soon married and, together with Aniuta, set off for Europe.

First the threesome tried Vienna, but it was too expensive to live there, and the mathematics seemed inferior to Sonya anyway.

Finally, it seemed best to split up. Aniuta settled in France, where she became active in political causes. Vladimir and Sonya moved to England, where they met Charles Darwin and Thomas Huxley. Sonya became good friends with the female novelist, George Elliot, whose biography Sonya later wrote.

It was in Germany, however, where Sonya accomplished her most significant work in mathematics. Fortunately, she received permission to attend mathematics and physics lectures at the University of Heidelberg. What she really wanted, though, was to study under the great scientist, R. W. Bunsen. Bunsen, who later invented the gas burner that bears his name, was vehemently opposed to higher education for women. He swore he would never let a woman into his laboratory.

Sonya Kovalevsky was small and slender, and looked younger than she was, but she was determined and persistent. Bunsen finally weakened in his stubborn refusal, allowing Kovalevsky to work with him in his lab for three terms, on the condition that she tell no other woman what she was doing. Surprisingly, they got along very well.

Kovalevsky tested her skills of persuasion again in Berlin. She moved there in hopes of studying under Karl Weierstrass, one of Germany's greatest mathematicians. He, too, had no interest in women students, but agreed to let Kovalevsky try.

"Here is a set of problems to get you started," he said. "Let me know if you have any trouble." Weierstrass deliberately gave Kovalevsky extremely difficult problems, hoping that she would quickly give up and move on.

Several days later, Kovalevsky returned to Weierstrass with the problems solved. When he saw her ingenious solutions, he realized that he had underestimated her, and soon accepted her as his private pupil. Weierstrass became the most important influence on Kovalevsky's development as a mathematician.

Weierstrass did all he could to get Kovalevsky a position teaching mathematics. Although she had graduated from university with honors, there were few places a woman could teach. Finally, she found a position at the University of Stockholm in Sweden. As the only woman professor in the country, Kovalevsky received many honors. Hundreds of couples named their baby girls Sonya.

In 1888, Sonya Kovalevsky read an announcement about the annual competition sponsored by the Paris Academy of Sciences. The *Prix Bordin* was the greatest prize offered for original work in mathematics. She had been working for some time on theories about Saturn's rings. This contest was just the incentive she needed to complete her studies. Throughout the entire summer Kovalevsky dedicated herself to research, computation, and writing. She pulled together everything she knew about physics and mathematics. Finally she was ready to submit her paper, "The Problem of the Rotation of a Solid Body About a Fixed Point."

Everyone entering the contest was given clear instructions. The entries were to be submitted without identification except for a motto of the contestant's choice written on the back. Each person was to write his or her name on a separate piece of paper, insert it into an envelope, seal it, and write the same motto on that envelope. This ensured absolute secrecy. The judges had no way of knowing whose work they were evaluating.

Finally, on Christmas Eve, the time for the announcement of the winner of the coveted prize had arrived. The official at the Academy cleared his throat and began to speak.

"Ladies and Gentlemen, welcome to this honored occasion. As you well know, the *Prix Bordin* is the most prestigious and valuable recognition awarded to mathematicians in Europe. This year I have the special privilege of announcing that, because of the exceptional quality and importance of our grand prize winning work, the Academy has decided to raise the cash award from 3000 to 5000 francs."

The crowd murmured in excitement. "Who do you suppose it could be?" "This must be really amazing!" "I'm glad I came to witness the ceremony this year!"

"As I was saying," the official continued, "the grand prize winner this year has solved an especially important problem. I'm sure you are all just as eager as I am to see which of our fine men has triumphed. The envelopes, please."

"On the back of the winning paper was this motto:

Say what you know,
Do what you must,
Come what may.

I shall now open the small envelope with the identical motto."

As the Academy spokesman pealed off the wax seal and pried open the envelope, a hush fell over the crowd. Everyone watched as he stared at the name in obvious disbelief. After a long pause, he began to smile. He cleared his throat and announced in a loud voice, "The winner is—Sonya Kovalevsky."

ALBERT EINSTEIN (YN-styn),1879–1955, was a theoretical physicist and a mathematical genius. Best known for developing the theory of relativity, he revolutionized thinking about time, space, mass, light, motion, and gravitation.

A Compass Points the Way

"What's that you're playing with, Albert?" asked Uncle Jacob.

"Father gave it to me. He says it's a compass."

"A compass, eh? What does it do?"

The five-year-old boy did not seem interested in conversation. He was engrossed in studying the circular object with its glass dial. He spun round and round, fascinated by the way the needle inside the compass turned with him.

"A compass points directions for travelers, Albert," said Uncle Jacob. "Are you planning a trip?"

Albert continued examining the intriguing gadget. Suddenly, he erupted with a string of questions for his uncle. "How can it be that the needle always knows where north is, Uncle Jacob? There must be something out there—something invisible—that is pulling it. Is that something also pulling me and you? How can there be something invisible in empty space?"

"Whoa! Slow down, Albert," laughed his uncle. "I'm only an engineer. I don't know the answers to all your questions, but I'll try to help you understand how it works."

A Compass Points the Way

Albert Einstein was glad his father had asked Uncle Jacob to work in their small electrical business, because Uncle Jacob had studied physics and mathematics. The fun-loving bachelor lived with Albert and his family, and often talked to Albert. Albert believed he could ask him almost any question.

When Albert was about ten years old, it was Uncle Jacob who asked the hard questions.

"How is it going at school, Albert?"

Albert fidgeted and looked down. "Okay, I guess."

His uncle knew that Albert did not like school. Several teachers had told Albert's parents that he would probably never amount to anything. When he should have been reciting his lessons, they said, he was daydreaming. Even the other boys were rude to him. They teased him because he was not good at sports.

"Uncle Jacob," said Albert, lifting his head. "Have you ever thought about how school is like the army? We have to go every day, wear uniforms, stand at attention when the teacher enters, and sit in neat rows. I hate the way they try to make us all into copies of each other."

"Well, I know how you feel about the military, Albert. I remember how frightened you used to be watching parades. When all the other little boys pretended to be soldiers, marching around with sticks on their shoulders, you ran away. But school is really not that bad, is it?"

"Almost. If I don't answer questions, I am scolded for not paying attention. But if I ask questions, my teachers say I am disrespectful," Albert complained. "Today, for example, we were supposed to learn about algebra. I didn't understand, and when I said so, I was told to be quiet and pay attention."

Jacob placed his hand on Albert's shoulder. "Let me tell you something about algebra. It's really very simple. Algebra is like this: when the animal we're hunting hasn't been caught, we temporarily call it x and continue to hunt it until it is bagged."

After that little talk, studying algebra became a game for Albert. Every day after school he and his uncle hunted for new ways to solve simple problems using algebra.

When he was twelve, Albert was given a book on geometry written by Euclid. This book fascinated him, and he quickly mastered the subject. He enjoyed the precise language and the proofs. The logical, orderly sequences were almost as pleasing as the beautiful Mozart sonatas he loved to play on his violin. Playing the violin helped Einstein relax; soon he found that geometry calmed him in the same way.

School was another story. When Einstein's family moved to Italy during his senior year in high school, he stayed behind to finish. But without the support and encouragement of his parents, he was miserable. At the suggestion of the school administrators, Einstein dropped out and joined his family in Italy.

Without a diploma, Einstein could not go to a university. There was a fine institute in Switzerland, however, that accepted students on the basis of an entrance exam. Einstein failed the test the first time because his scores in language and biology were so poor. But because the officials were so impressed by his excellent performance on the mathematics sections, they encouraged him to try again. After an enjoyable senior year in the more relaxed Swiss system, Einstein passed the test and went on to the Polytechnic Institute in Zurich.

He decided to support himself by teaching physics, but finding a teaching job was very difficult. First of all, there was some prejudice against him because he was both German and Jewish. Also, his interviewers could tell that Einstein wasn't really interested in teaching. His first love was research.

Some people thought Einstein was just plain strange. He didn't care much about making money, and he didn't care how he looked or whether his hair was combed. He was used to saying what he thought, even if it sounded impolite. It was especially hard for such an honest and outspoken person to get a teaching position.

Finally, Einstein accepted a job in the patent office in Bern, Switzerland. His assignment was to examine new inventions and evaluate their merits. Those that seemed worthwhile were issued patents. While this work was not exactly boring, it was a little tedious. It did, however, give Einstein time to think and to work on his own research. While he was working in the patent office he began to put together a theory that revolutionized the way people thought about the universe.

Einstein did not have close contact with other scientists and did not study the latest literature, but he had read about experiments on the speed of light. He believed that light speed was constant, and that everything else, like time and space, was relative, not absolute. In his complex theory of relativity, Einstein showed that time varied, depending on motion or speed. He published a series of papers on this and related topics in 1905.

During the next ten years, Einstein continued to develop applications of this breakthrough in the understanding of light and time. His famous equation, $E = mc^2$, clarified his understanding of how closely energy and matter are related. In this equation, E represents the energy in any particle of matter, m represents the mass of the particle, and c stands for the speed of light. His proof that matter could be changed into energy led to the development of atomic energy and, ultimately, the atomic bomb.

Einstein became not only famous, but also controversial. His new ideas threatened many scientists, who had other ways of viewing the physical universe. But Einstein was not bothered by public opinion, caring much more for the discovery of scientific truth. The challenge to describe complicated processes in nature with simple mathematical formulas never dimmed for Einstein. He was convinced that if science was to progress, people had to be willing to ask questions. When an interviewer asked him how he had shaped his theory of relativity, he responded, "I challenged an axiom." Questioning current beliefs (*including his own*) should never be discouraged, he said.

In 1921 Einstein received the Nobel Prize in Physics for his earlier work on the law of the photoelectric effect. This law explains how and why special metals emit electrons after light falls on their surfaces. It is not considered Einstein's most important work, but it may be his least controversial.

Einstein loved searching for scientific truth for its own sake, but he soon came to realize that the practical application of his work could not be avoided. As an adult, he disliked military force just as much as he had in childhood, and he was always eager to help people find peaceful solutions to their disagreements. When Germany became an aggressor and attempted to control Europe, naturally he was upset. To show his concern, he renounced his German citizenship and became a Swiss citizen.

Einstein was visiting the United States at the time Hitler gained power in Germany. He cringed as he watched Hitler develop sinister racial and political policies. Einstein believed Hitler would use anyone and anything to further his cause. All German scientists were expected to contribute to his efforts to conquer the world. When Einstein refused, Hitler put a price on his head.

Einstein had been teaching at the University of Berlin. When he realized that his Swiss citizenship would not protect him from Hitler's plot to have him killed, he resigned and moved to the United States. "I will stay in a country only where political liberty, toleration, and equality of all citizens before the law are the rule," he said. He was offered a position at the Institute for Advanced Study at Princeton University. In 1934 he became a United States citizen.

Soon it became apparent that German scientists were close to developing the powerful atomic bomb. Einstein was nervous about this. It wasn't good to have that much power in the hands of a society that might misuse it. In 1939 he wrote a letter to President Franklin Roosevelt explaining how the bomb could be made, and suggesting it be used by the United States to maintain peace in the world. He hoped that the United States would demonstrate the bomb by dropping it in an uninhabited region. Perhaps when other nations saw its power, they would be more willing to negotiate for peace.

Six years later, when the United States dropped the first atomic bomb on Hiroshima, Einstein was deeply grieved. He felt responsible for the tremendous devastation and death caused by the bomb. He had never wanted atomic power to be used as a means of destruction. Now he regretted ever writing to Roosevelt. For the rest of his life, he worked for world peace through a variety of organizations.

One of Einstein's dreams was the creation of the nation Israel as the Jewish homeland. He offered his advice and support to this effort. In 1948 the dream of millions of people became reality as Israel declared its statehood. When Einstein was invited to be the second President of Israel, he declined the offer. An interviewer asked him why. He responded, "Scientific problems are familiar to me, but I have neither the natural capacity nor the necessary experience to handle human beings."

As Einstein grew older, many people came to know and love him. Stories about his absentmindedness as a scientist at Princeton became almost legendary. He often forgot where he lived, and would have to stop people who looked familiar on campus to ask directions. When he did find his street, he couldn't tell one house from the other. To prevent this frequent embarrassment, he had his front door painted bright red!

Einstein especially loved children. They didn't care if he went without socks or walked in the rain without an umbrella. Sometimes he helped the neighborhood children with their mathematics, but most of the time he just played with them. To children, he was famous not because he was a great mathematician and scientist, but because he could wiggle his ears.

People of all ages have benefited from Einstein's great formulas, but for young people, he left another formula.

"Where x stands for hard work, y stands for play, and z stands for knowing when to listen, $x + y + z =$ success."

GEORGE PÓLYA (POL-yuh), 1887–1985, was a Hungarian mathematician who immigrated to the United States in 1940. He is best known for his work in problem solving, and he profoundly influenced the way mathematics is taught.

The Master Problem Solver

The last seconds of the game ticked away. "Kick it over here, George!"

"Laszlo," shouted George, "watch out behind you! Go for the goal!"

George Pólya jumped and cheered as his younger brother chipped the ball into the goal. When the referee blew the final whistle, George was the first to reach his brother and lift him into the air. He carried him on his shoulders as the victorious team surrounded them.

"You did it, Laszlo. You broke the tie and won it for us!" Their teammate Julius offered to help George with his load, but George broke into a dance-like run, effortlessly carrying Laszlo around the field.

"Laszlo may be the better soccer player, but George is sure stronger," Julius commented to the other players. "Look how easily he carries his brother, and Laszlo is so much taller. He must also be heavy."

"Yeah," said one of his teammates. "They say George rearranges the furniture in the house every night—with one hand—just to stay in shape."

George Pólya *was* strong. He used his strength and energy in soccer and wrestling. But there are many ways to be strong. Perhaps Pólya's greatest strength was his stubborn determination to solve whatever problems he faced.

Pólya had more than his share of problems. His father died when he was ten, and he missed the security of a loving father. He and Laszlo often argued and fought, with their mother usually supporting the younger Laszlo. George was naturally mischievous, and rebelled against authority by occasionally running away from home. Usually he just went for a long walk to explore the streets of his native Budapest.

In high school, George worked hard, but he resented the emphasis on memorization. It seemed like every spare minute was used up memorizing some poem or the conjugation of a verb.

George's Uncle Armin had an idea. "George, why don't you enter the national competition in mathematics? I think you could do very well. Maybe you could earn a scholarship for college."

"It's kind of you to say so, Uncle Armin, but I really don't care for mathematics. I think I'll study languages, or law like my father."

"Oh, those are good subjects," Uncle Armin agreed. "But George, you love to solve problems. I think you'd be happier in mathematics."

Partly to satisfy his uncle, Pólya signed up for the competition, one of the most prestigious contests in Hungary. The winning students often went on to develop successful careers in mathematics and science.

During the test, Pólya must have become either frustrated or bored, because he never handed in his booklet. Chances for a future in mathematics certainly looked doubtful, so George enrolled at the University of Budapest to study law.

"You know," said Pólya one day to his brother, "the law is full of legal technicalities. I feel so discouraged by having to memorize them. It really weighs me down."

Laszlo was sympathetic. "I can understand that. What are you going to do about it?"

"Well, I've been thinking. My professor of biology is an interesting teacher. It's made me think about trying that field myself."

Pólya changed his major to biology. Before long, he tired of that, too, and switched again to language and literature. This time he'd found a subject he did well in. He completed the program, earning the right to teach Latin and Hungarian in the lower grades.

But Pólya was still dissatisfied with his education. Instead of giving up, he began to take some courses in philosophy, and found himself intrigued with the ideas. Noticing his exceptional ability to reason and think logically, his professor suggested Pólya take some courses in physics and mathematics to build on this strength.

It was a mathematics course taught by Lipot Fejer that determined Pólya's career. Here was a teacher unlike any he had ever met, one with a charming personality and a great sense of humor. He also seemed to really care about his students. Some evenings Fejer joined them at a coffee house, and they would talk and laugh together.

"I have finally figured myself out," Pólya told Laszlo one day. "I am not good enough for physics and I am too good for philosophy. Mathematics, being right in the middle, is where I belong."

He had also learned that teachers play an important role in determining whether or not one will enjoy a subject. "The most interesting topic," he often said, "can be made boring by a poor teacher."

Once Pólya realized how much he enjoyed mathematics, he completed his education with enthusiasm. In 1912 he earned a doctorate in mathematics from the University of Budapest.

After graduate school, Pólya spent one year studying in Vienna. To help pay his expenses at the university, he accepted an assignment as a tutor for the young son of a baron. Each week he met with Gregor and tried to help him understand mathematics and science.

"I am very frustrated," Pólya confided to a friend over coffee. "For some reason, Gregor is making little progress. No matter how hard I try, he does not see what to do to solve his problems."

Pólya made up his mind to find a way to help Gregor. For hours, he rehearsed explaining the geometry problem in new ways to Gregor. He tried to recall the patterns and the essential ideas he used when he solved the problem himself. Finally, he came up with a sketch of the process used to solve problems. This was an exciting discovery for Pólya, and it began his lifelong interest in problem solving.

He set to work to describe *how* to solve problems, not just for Gregor, but for all students like him. Most of Pólya's teachers had stressed memorization. Certain procedures should be applied to specific kinds of problems, they said. If one couldn't remember which procedure to use, failure was certain. Pólya thought there must be a better way.

Shortly after Pólya finished his formal education, he was invited to Zurich, Switzerland, to teach at a technical institute. He found lodging at an inexpensive but pleasant hotel near some beautiful woods. This suited Pólya perfectly. He loved walking. Here, he could work hard at the institute and then relax with a long walk in the woods. In between, he sometimes stopped to play dominoes with an elderly gentleman who also lived at the hotel. Since the older man couldn't get out much, he was delighted with Pólya's company.

Usually when Pólya knocked on the door, Mr. Weber boomed in a loud voice for him to come in. One day, Pólya was shocked when a beautiful young woman opened the door instead. When she saw the surprised look on his face, she blushed.

"George," announced Mr. Weber. "I'd like you to meet my daughter, Stella." The two young people smiled shyly and shook hands. "Stella, this is that fine young mathematician I've been talking about!"

Pólya and Stella met several times at Mr. Weber's apartment, and often walked together in the woods. They were married in 1918, and shared sixty-seven years. Stella was an intelligent woman and a gracious hostess. She was also an amateur photographer. When other mathematicians came to visit, Stella always remembered the camera. For many years, Pólya delighted in showing their collection of photographs to visitors and friends.

One day, after the Pólyas were married, George went for one of his beloved walks through the woods. It was a beautiful morning. The sun filtered lightly through the trees. He walked briskly, occasionally tapping the path with a stick. Suddenly, as he came around an overgrown shrub, Pólya nearly bumped into a young man and woman embracing. Everyone was embarrassed, and Pólya began to apologize.

"I was so caught up with the splendor of the morning," he explained, suddenly recognizing the young man as one of his students. "I didn't even see you."

The young man quickly regained his composure, and introduced his fiancée to Dr. Pólya. "Dr. Pólya is my professor at the Institute of Technology," he said.

After more mumbled apologies and courteous good-byes, Pólya went on his way and the couple resumed their walk, in a different direction. The professor was a kind and friendly gentleman, but the couple wanted to be alone.

About twenty minutes later, Pólya cringed as he rounded a bend in the path. It was the young lovers again, coming towards him. Would they think he was spying on them? Pólya tipped his hat, smiled, and kept going. The couple blushed and stared at him. Although they kept choosing new paths and alternate directions, the two parties ran into each other *five* times during one morning's walk in the woods.

Later, Pólya related the story to Stella.

"What do you suppose my young student and his fiancée think of me, Stella?"

"Oh, don't worry about it, dear," she consoled. "They're probably too much in love to notice you, or anyone else."

"That's true. Remember how we loved disappearing down those paths when we were getting to know each other?" He touched Stella's hand and smiled. "But I would never deliberately spy on a courting couple, or on anyone else for that matter. The network of paths through the woods is quite complex and spread out. I can't understand how I could have run into them so many times!"

Pólya continued to ponder the incident. What was the likelihood of meeting the couple that often by accident? This experience led Pólya to study what he later called the *random walk* problem. He imagined a modern city of perfectly square blocks. Half the streets would run east and west and the other half north and south. Given any one intersection of streets as the starting point, one could move in any of four directions. If the choice of direction at each intersection thereafter were purely random, what was the probability of returning to the starting point?

Pólya was the first person to study this problem. Several years later he published a paper proving that if the walk continued long enough, one was certain to return to the starting point.

Pólya was a gentle, loving man, who tried not to offend anyone. The political tensions preceding World War II grieved him. He was sorry that some people were abused just because of their ethnic backgrounds. His own brother, Jeno, was executed because he was Jewish, although Pólya did not learn of his death until several years later.

The Pólyas decided to move to the United States, and Dr. Pólya was invited to teach at Stanford University. He and Stella both loved their new community and quickly made friends with other professors and their families, as well as with many students.

Pólya's most famous book, *How to Solve It*, was published in English in 1945. This practical guide to problem solving was eventually translated into fifteen languages and sold more than a million copies.

Pólya continued to do original research in a variety of mathematical fields. He published many articles and several books in Europe and while at Stanford. He became best known for his helpful insights into problem solving. To solve a problem, he said, look at concrete examples and check for patterns. If a problem is too hard, "wish for" an easier one, and then observe how that one is solved. He believed the solving process was more important than the solution. Pólya taught students to experiment—to be willing to make a guess and then test it out. "It is better to solve one problem five different ways," he often reminded them, "than to solve five different problems."

Pólya decided that too many of his students did not know how to begin to solve problems. "I have a dream," he told his colleagues at Stanford. "I want to show teachers how to help their students solve problems. I want to inspire them to make mathematics exciting and satisfying for their students!"

After most professors his age had retired, George Pólya developed a program to help teachers teach mathematics more effectively. Thousands came during their summer vacations to learn from this master teacher. They found a man who was not only a great mathematician, but also a wonderful friend. More than anything else, they praised him for the way he modeled the excitement of mathematical discovery. He was never so happy as when he stood in front of a class, leading students step by step to a surprisingly simple solution.

Resource List

◆

Abbott, David. *The Biographical Dictionary of Scientists: Mathematicians.* New York: Peter Bedrick Books, 1986.

Beckman, Petr. *A History of Pi.* New York: St. Martin's Press, 1971.

Bedini, Silvio A. *The Life of Benjamin Banneker.* Rancho Cordova, Calif.: Landmark Enterprises, 1972.

Bell, E.T. *Men of Mathematics.* New York: Simon and Schuster, 1965.

Boyer, Carl B. and Uta Merzbach. *A History of Mathematics.* New York: John Wiley and Sons, 1989.

Burton, David M. *The History of Mathematics.* Boston: Allyn and Bacon, 1985.

Dunham, William. *Journey Through Genius: The Great Theorems of Mathematics.* New York: John Wiley and Sons, 1990.

Edeen, Susan, and John Edeen. *Portraits for Classroom Bulletin Boards: Mathematicians. Books 1* and 2 and *Women Mathematicians.* Palo Alto, Calif.: Dale Seymour Publications, 1988.

Eves, Howard W. *An Introduction to the History of Mathematics.* 6th ed. New York: Saunders College Publishing, 1990.

_______. *In Mathematical Circles.* Vols. 1 and 2. Boston: Prindle, Weber and Schmidt, 1969.

Garland, Trudi. *Fascinating Fibonaccis.* Palo Alto, Calif.: Dale Seymour Publications, 1987.

Gies, Joseph, and Frances Gies. *Leonard of Pisa and the New Mathematics of the Middle Ages*. Gainesville, Ga.: New Classics Library, 1983.

Grinstein, Louise S., and Paul J. Campbell. *Women of Mathematics: A Biobibliographic Sourcebook*. New York: Greenwood Press, 1987.

Hollingdale, Stuart. *Makers of Mathematics*. New York: Penguin Books, 1989.

Johnson, Arthur. *Classic Math: History Topics for the Classroom*. Palo Alto, Calif.: Dale Seymour Publications, 1994.

Katz, Victor J. *A History of Mathematics*. New York: Harper Collins, 1993.

Kramer, Edna E. *The Nature and Growth of Modern Mathematics*. Princeton: Princeton University Press, 1981.

Multiculturalism in Mathematics, Science, and Technology. Menlo Park, Calif.: Addison-Wesley, 1993.

Historical Topics for the Mathematics Classroom. Reston, Va.: NCTM, 1989.

Ore, Oystein. *Niels Henrik Abel: Mathematician Extraordinary*. New York: Chelsea Publishing Company, 1974.

Osen, Lynn M. *Women in Mathematics*. Cambridge, Mass.: MIT Press, 1974.

Perl, Teri. *Math Equals: Biographies of Women Mathematicians*. Menlo Park, Calif.: Addison-Wesley, 1978.

Perl, Teri. *Women and Numbers*. San Carlos, Calif.: Wide World Publishing, 1993.

Reimer, Luetta, and Wilbert Reimer. *Mathematicians Are People, Too*. Vol. 1. Palo Alto, Calif.: Dale Seymour Publications, 1990.

Reimer, Wilbert, and Luetta Reimer. *Historical Connections in Mathematics: Resources for Using History of Mathematics in the Classroom.* Vols. 1, 2, and 3. Fresno, Calif.: AIMS Education Foundation, 1992, 1993, 1995.

Schaaf, William. *Mathematics and Science: An Adventure in Postage Stamps.* Reston, Va.: NCTM, 1978.

Stillwell, John. *Mathematics and Its History.* New York: Springer-Verlag, 1989.

Struik, Dirk J. *A Concise History of Mathematics.* 4th ed. New York: Dover, 1987.

Taylor, Harold, and Loretta Taylor. *George Pólya: Master of Discovery.* Palo Alto, Calif.: Dale Seymour Publications, 1993.

Turnbull, Herbert W. *The Great Mathematicians.* New York: New York University Press, 1961.

Glossary

◆

abacus

An ancient calculating machine still used in Eastern countries to aid in arithmetic computation. Made of beads strung on wires or dowels fastened into a frame.

algebra

The branch of mathematics that uses special symbols, such as letters, to express relationships among numbers.

almanac

A book or table containing a calendar of days, weeks, and months, to which astronomical data and various statistics are often added, such as the times of sunset and sunrise, phases of the moon, or tides.

analytic geometry

The geometry in which position is represented analytically (by coordinates) and algebraic methods of reasoning are used.

analysis

The area of mathematics that uses the methods of algebra and calculus.

astrology

The study of the presumed relationship between the position of heavenly bodies, primarily the planets, and events or human personality.

astronomical clock
A precise timepiece, set according to the sun, used in eighteenth century surveying.

astronomy
The science that deals with the study of the sun, moon, stars, planets, and other heavenly bodies.

axiom
A statement accepted as true without proof, also called a postulate.

calculus
The branch of mathematics that deals with rates of change such as velocity and acceleration, maximums and minimums, areas, volumes, and many other related topics.

chemistry
The science that studies all kinds of substances to learn what they are made of, what characteristics they have, and what kinds of changes occur when they combine with other substances.

conics or conic sections
The curves formed when a plane intersects a right circular cone. They are the circle, ellipse, parabola, and hyperbola.

coordinate system
A Cartesian coordinate system (named after Descartes) uses perpendicular lines as reference lines to identify points by sets of numbers.

cubic equation (also known as third degree equation)
An equation whose highest term is cubed such as $x^3 + 2x^2 - 6x + 4 = 0$.

differential equation
A special kind of equation studied in calculus.

eclipse
The apparent dimming or elimination of light from one planet or celestial body caused when another body passes in front of it.

ephemeris
A table identifying the positions of a celestial body at regular intervals.

Euclid's *Elements*
Euclid's most famous work, consisting of thirteen books, was an organized collection of all mathematical knowledge up to his time. For more than 2000 years, translations of some books of *Elements* were used as school textbooks.

Euclid's Fifth Postulate
The most famous of Euclid's postulates. It states that through a point not on a given line, one and only one line can be drawn parallel to the given line.

equation
A statement saying that two expressions are equal.

Fibonacci sequence
A sequence of numbers, each one being the sum of the two numbers before it. These numbers form a pattern not only in mathematics but in nature.

The first ten terms of the sequence are 1, 1, 2, 3, 5, 8, 13, 21, 34, and 55.

fifth degree equation
An equation whose highest term is a fifth degree term such as $x^5 + 2x^4 - 7x^3 + 2x^2 - 5x + 4 = 0$.

formula
A general rule stated in mathematical language.

fourth degree equation
An equation whose highest term is a fourth degree term such as $5x^4 - 6x^3 + 3x^2 - 2x + 9 = 0$.

geometry
The branch of mathematics that deals with shape, size, symmetry, and other properties of figures.

group theory
The study of mathematical systems (called *groups*) that satisfy specific conditions. A group is a set of elements and a rule for combining any two of those elements to get another element of the set; each group must have an identity element, and each element must have an inverse.

Hindu-Arabic numerals
The number symbols 1, 2, 3, 4, 5, 6, 7, 8, 9. These originated in India and were introduced into Europe by the Arabs.

imaginary numbers
Numbers arising from the square root of certain negative numbers, such as $\sqrt{-1}$, $\sqrt{-5}$, etc.

imaginary roots
A solution of an equation that is an imaginary number.

integer
Any positive or negative whole number or zero. The following are examples of integers: −32, 16, 0, 2001.

linear equation
A first degree equation, such as $3x + 6 = 15$.

logarithm or log
The exponent of a number when that number is written as a power of a fixed number, called the base. The logarithm of 100 using 10 as the base is 2 since $10^2 = 100$. It is written $\log_{10} 100 = 2$. Logarithms were widely used before calculators were introduced to simplify multiplication by reducing it to addition.

negative numbers
Numbers less than 0, such as −2, −3.5, −10.

number theory
The study of the properties of integers, including factoring, dividing, prime numbers, and related subjects.

Pascal's triangle
A triangular array of numbers created by beginning and ending each row with 1. Every other number is obtained by adding the two numbers in the preceding row closest to it.

```
            1
          1   1
        1   2   1
      1   3   3   1
    1   4   6   4   1
  1   5  10  10   5   1
1   6  15  20  15   6   1
```

physics
The science that deals with matter and energy and the laws governing them. Physics studies motion, light, heat, sound, electricity, and force.